ABOUT THE AUTHOR

Jaki Scarcello has spent 30 years listening to and supporting
individuals and organizations as a leadership consultant,
facilitator, and coach working with Fortune 500 companies
in Canada and the United States. She lives a nomadic life
with two fixed bases—Toronto and Hermosa Beach, California.
Between spells in either home she travels with her husband—
a writer and teacher.

www.fiftyfab.com

50

and fabulous

life-affirming lessons from women
aged 45 to 102

Jaki Scarcello

Originally published in 2010.
This edition first published in the UK and USA 2014 by
Watkins Publishing Limited
PO Box 883, Oxford OX1 9PL, UK
A member of Osprey Group

For enquiries in the USA and Canada:
Osprey Publishing
PO Box 3985, New York NY 10185-3985
Tel: (001) 212 753 4402
Email: info@ospreypublishing.com

1 3 5 7 9 10 8 6 4 2
Designed and typeset by Gail Jones
Printed and bound by CPI Group (UK) Ltd, Croydon, CR0 4YY

A CIP record for this book is available from the British Library
ISBN: 978-1-78028-754-6

Watkins Publishing is supporting the Woodland Trust,
the UK's leading woodland conservation charity, by funding tree-
planting initiatives and woodland maintenance.

www.watkinspublishing.co.uk

ACKNOWLEDGMENTS

Thank you, Grand Dames of the Harvest. You opened your hearts and lives to me and shared the treasured secrets of your amazing life 50+. This book would obviously not exist without you and I would never have discovered the joy that awaits us as we age. I will be forever grateful for your insights.

Thank you also to all those "sparkly" older women who have crossed in and out of my life and fascinated and intrigued me enough to set me on this quest to understand what was in those eyes I loved so much.

Thank you to Michael Mann at Watkins Publishing. You have been a supporter and a tolerant publisher from day one, and you have, even with my endless questions, maintained a "gud mud." I am humbled by your faith in what I had to say in these pages.

I also thank the fine operation at Watkins for the gift of Anne Barthel, my editor. Her magic and skill has crafted this book. I can think of no more skilled hands, mind, or heart into which I could entrust my words.

Thank you also to Penny Stopa for being there on my journey to this book.

Thank you to my cheering squad: Lizanne, for the shelter of your home and for your courage that is proof of the existence of spirit in our lives. Dorothy, for bringing me the words of the oldest interviewee with great skill and through your own wisdom. Pat, for examples that enhanced the stories of the Women of the Harvest. John L. and Katherine for your interest and encouragement. You have all supported my dream that the words of the Women of the Harvest may bring joy and comfort to the lives of others.

To Emily and Michelle, for the permission to pick your brains and for the hearts you threw in for nothing.

To Sue, my creative muse, for her endless encouragement and incredible, creative role modeling. I am so glad you liked my suit.

Thank you to Ethel, who was my most pragmatic supporter. "Just write the darn thing," she said to me, more than once. Without your friendship I would not be the person I am today.

To Rebecca, whose diligent pursuit of publication permissions gave me time I desperately needed as the deadline loomed.

To Andrea for her creativity à la carte.

To Tara for her graphics consulting. I am proud you

are my daughter and relieved because I could never afford what your talent is worth.

To Brian for the thoughtful gift of the notebook in which this book first started to form. It is not the first time your kindness has been just what I needed.

To Tessa, my mentor and role model, and to all at BTW, thank you for the inspiration and the energy and the monthly reminder that age is purely a state of mind.

To Nacho and his kitchen table, where much of this book was crafted. You run a fabulous writer's retreat house.

To Sharda, whose grace and elegance in age is a message all its own.

Finally, to my husband, Wayne, who was the first to make me believe I could actually do this. Your faith in my ability means so much more because of the respect I have for yours. Thank you and much love to you always.

And always to Ramesh Balsekar . . .

In loving memory of my parents
who taught me that all is possible and change is the way of life

To Tara and Brian who are proof that all is possible and my love
for whom is the only constant I know

CONTENTS

In the depth of winter
I finally learned that
there was in me
an invincible summer.

Albert Camus

A NOTE
TO
My Reader

A few years ago I began to interview interesting women who were nearing or passing the age of 50. I started the project for a variety of reasons, in response to circumstances in my professional life as a corporate and executive coach and in response to questions that arose in my personal life. By the time I stopped asking questions, I had interviewed women between the ages of 45 and 102, from five countries. At the end of the interviews, I knew I needed to write these women's stories. My enthusiasm came from a desire to share what they had shared with me, along with a strong sense that others—both individuals and our society— needed to hear what I had discovered and needed to hear it soon.

As the interviews progressed, I had discerned that women facing their fiftieth birthdays and/or the event of menopause fall into two categories:

- Those who are horrified by their aging, who look out on their future as a time of decline and diminishing capacity to be postponed and denied as long as possible.

- Those who aren't fazed by the physical milestone of menopause or the chronological significance of turning 50, but who celebrate the new possibilities each stage of their lives brings.

These women, whom I call the Women of the Harvest, are not oblivious to the changes happening in their lives. They have simply embraced the idea that being over 50 and female at this time in history is an opportunity richer and more ripe with potential than ever before.

I believed that what I had discovered about those who celebrated this season of life was too significant not to be shared and that everyone should hear what they had to say. In my excitement and naïveté I believed everyone would listen. I failed to notice how some people seemed to nod off instead. Then one day, when my husband and I were having lunch with some friends, one of them asked how my book was coming along. Another dear friend perked up with interest. "Oh, what are you writing about?" he asked.

"The value to society of a woman over 50," I answered. Okay, it was not a very good description of my subject, but I was trying to summarize and I had not yet perfected my "elevator speech."

"Value of a woman over 50!" he responded. "Less, less value, way down," he groaned, with a hand gesture that signaled plummeting stock.

He is a bright young guy, 45, gay, and very European. I love him. He is funny and full of life as only a hyperactive Spaniard could be. Yet here he was telling me and my sisters—oh, yes, in my indignation I assumed instantaneous solidarity with every woman 50 and over— that we had less value today just because of our age. Our age, an accident of our birth dates!

I had a drawer full of interviews that screamed liar! at him.

My husband, playing the unofficial agent role, countered, "There is a great market for this book. Women over 50 are the biggest book consumers in the U.S." *Only one problem*, I thought to myself. *I am not writing because there is a market.*

A professional writer would do this because she actually knew how to and intended to make money from her craft. But I am some sort of delusional idealist who thinks she has a responsibility to share this really great news she's discovered about this amazing unstudied and unconquered time in a woman's life, come on, load the wagons, let's go!

As lunch wound down, I was left with this question: did anyone really care about this news that I had such a burning desire to print, or was writing a book about the value of older women, for the purpose of convincing the world that 75 and female is just as good as 25 and female, a sort of visionary *hara-kiri?*

Then I realized that to have any chance of "growing up" to be like one of these amazing women I had interviewed, I had to act like one, starting now. I just had to proceed with my efforts to share their wisdom.

Since then I have come to terms with my "market," as my husband puts it. This book is not for everyone. If you have picked it up, chances are you're one of the following:

- **a woman over 50**

- **a woman approaching 50**

🌹 a woman who knows a woman over 50 or
approaching 50 who needs some cheering up

🌹 an aspiring writer who saw the title and thought,
Wow, if they would publish this, I have a chance.

I accept this. I accept you as my readers and I am
thrilled to have you here, ready to hear about the harvest
season of a woman's life.

I do think there are some other folks who could benefit
from reading this book; it's short, sweet, and quickly
consumed. Perhaps not so quickly digested, but you can
take something for that. So when you finish reading the
volume in your hand, please pass it on to someone outside
the original readership cohort. May I suggest:

🌹 Share it with a younger woman in the prime of her
productive years, working 50 to 60 hours a week
building an amazing career, managing the growth
and development of a couple of super kids, and
keeping the fires hot and fun with the great guy she
fell for a decade or two ago. She is tired, she begs for
elusive balance in her life, and she probably thinks

old means over . . . perhaps in these pages she will be able to see that her future promises more than she can imagine.

Donate your copy to one of those newly minted young MBAs who sit next to you at work. You know, the ones with all the answers and all the opinions who have not yet learned to listen, who don't realize that what they learned in school was out of date twelve months before they graduated and that if they don't start to listen to what is going on around them they will never be able to keep up. This is not a judgment; it is a description of a stage in life. There is wisdom and perspective in the voices of the Women of the Harvest for these young women or men.

Rush back to the store as many copies as you can and give them to every man you know who lives with a woman over 50. Tell him, "This is who she is, this woman you are still in love with after all these years, and this is the place where she lives now." He will appreciate the help, really.

As I worked on this project, I spoke to many women celebrating their harvest seasons in many inspiring and empowering ways, but this work is not a research project. I did not conduct empirical studies; I talked with women. In these pages I mix the wisdom they shared with me with observations, intuitions, and none too few opinions of my own.

Being over 50 and female at this time in history is an opportunity richer and more ripe with potential than ever before.

You are free to agree or disagree, but do not seek to prove or disprove these statements. It will frustrate you and probably me, and it is not necessary. If anything I offer resonates with you, please take it into your life and use it in any way that helps. If what I say does not resonate, then leave it here and perhaps the next person to come by will see it differently.

Maybe over time word will get out and other women will become curious about the harvest season in their lives. Folks will line up to hear women like the ones I have interviewed talk about the secret of loving just what and where you are. Until then, I intend to follow the advice of one of my interviewees when she had this to say about conventional wisdom:

"It is the wisdom of the majority, and by the time the idea is accepted by the majority it is out of date. You see, there is nothing to be gained by waiting for the rest of the world to see things as I do."

INTRODUCTION:
Women of the Harvest

On the wall of a major department store in a large North American city, there is a billboard with a picture of a Barbie doll. These words are printed beside the picture:

"I am turning fifty . . . don't tell anyone."

This is what we are up against, ladies. Why is Barbie afraid to let her 50 years out of the plastic bag? Her figure is not changing; there is not a hint of wrinkle on that molded face. This is the ultimate ridiculousness: a woman who cannot possibly get cellulite, whose breasts are permanently propped up, and whose underarms you can write on because they will never jiggle . . . wants to hide her age.

Between the lines of this frivolous ad is an insidious message aimed at women: *If you are old now, that's bad, and you should hide it. If you are young now, one day you will be old, and that will be bad too, so maybe start hiding it now.* Could this explain 30-year-olds lining up for Botox?

In the same city, a woman well over 50 was having a drink in a restaurant when a younger woman walked up to her and said, "I just had to tell you you are a beautiful woman. My friend and I were just talking about the new face women—you know the ones—and how silly that is. Look at you, you look amazing." "New face women" was a reference to faces after plastic surgery.

The older woman was not oblivious to the fact that she was being congratulated for having wrinkles and gray hair and, she believed, for having the guts to flaunt them, but she took that compliment anyway, and here is why.

She had never had a complete stranger walk up to her in public and offer her a compliment, even in her 20s or 30s. She began to think there was something positive to this aging thing, and she felt great about who she had grown up to be.

What gave her the most pleasure was not the ego boost but the knowledge that she had been a role model for that younger woman. She had stated, with her style and grace, by smiling and laughing and sitting proudly in her clothes, that it is okay to be just the way you are. This, she believed, was the beauty the younger woman saw—something that shines right through the saggy stuff.

In the pursuit of eternal youth, everyone loses. A woman loses the gifts of age, society loses the wisdom of the mature woman, and youth loses the hope of a deeper future.

As women fight to stop the natural forces of the physical universe, they rob themselves and those around them of the psychological and emotional benefits that aging provides. While they seek to stop time, or at least trick it, by duplicating some earlier stage of life, they fail to embrace a season in which the fruits of a life lived—not well or poorly lived but simply lived—are ready to gather in. Unlike the material rewards of our societies, which are often reserved for those we define as worthy, these fruits are available to all who reach for them. This time in a woman's life is a time of grace, an unmerited gift from God.

In the pursuit of eternal youth, everyone loses. A woman loses the gifts of age, society loses the wisdom of the mature woman, and youth loses the hope of a deeper future.

We all know at least one woman who does not seek eternal youth, who has not turned her postmenopausal years into a desperate and eventually futile attempt to erase "herstory." We see her and we ask ourselves, does she know something the rest of us do not? Is she finding one more way to swim against the tide? Or is she just a fool who doesn't get that youth will always be best? Most maddening of all, why does she look so joyful, light, and alive?

This woman, and women like her—these are the ones I have sought out to listen to what they can tell us about life and living at 50+.

Fifty plus. That little mathematical cross means so much more than the number 50 plus one, two, or three. It seems it really does mean 50 plus *more*—plus this wisdom, plus that courage, plus these possibilities, even this undercurrent of peace—plus, plus, plus. This is what I've learned from the women who have shared their stories with me, and this is how I'll ask you to rethink the images of age as you move through this book: age means plus, +, not less but more.

Our societies need these women now more than ever as the practices and standards of the past decades are thrown up in the air and we are freefalling into a new way of living. Now that I think about it, that last statement is an attribute of aging in itself; I suppose that every generation upon reaching the 50+ years has judged its times as "a-changing." So maybe the real point is that change is life's reality, but one we humans are inconveniently not good at handling. We often seek stability first and ways to stop the tide of change. By 50 we should have some inkling that stopping the tides is a task we are not up to. If we observe the folks around us who seem most content, happy, and successful at the living game, we will see that they have put their energy into being part of what is new and uniquely molding that flow of change. In their freefall to the new ways, whatever they perceive them to be, they have found and used natural resources of wisdom and energy that, ironically, change in life provides to us all.

My interviews with the Women of the Harvest are a sort of anthropological study, field notes on the heretofore unstudied celebrants of the harvest season. Unlike the work of some well-meaning explorers in undiscovered cultures, my publication of my findings will not destroy their way of life. But knowing them will bring the rest of us knowledge to enrich our lives and the world in which we live.

Sharing these women's inner world is not a thinly veiled attempt to get our children to finally listen to their mothers, or to get our partners to eventually admit we're right, or even to bully our sisters into improved self-respect. You can accuse me of all those motives, but truly they are not mine. I have simply found a woman we should celebrate, one who moves against the tide but also turns it, one whose wisdom needs its moment in the sun (with sunscreen, of course).

Why the Women of the Harvest? Because it fits in every possible way. Harvest, as a season, is not an ending but a time to celebrate the yield brought forth from work and care and the simple passage of time. Harvest is the opposite of barren in my thesaurus.

At harvest time, the fruits of the field are distributed to nurture the harvester and the community. Except for a harvest feast or two, mostly the harvest is darn hard work. It is also one of the few stages of farm work when farmers are content in that very time, that very moment of the growth cycle. Earlier, they worried over seeds until they sprouted; young plants needed protection from drought and disease and the ripe fruit needed to be netted to keep it from the birds. But the harvest is the perfect time, and no true farmer would wish to be anywhere but right there, knee deep in the crop of the season.

The Women of the Harvest are celebrating too, just celebrating what they are today, be it at 50 or 75 or 98. This is not the kind of celebration that involves just sipping champagne, nibbling canapés, and flaunting your newest silks. I mean a *real* harvest celebration . . . work.

Harvest, as a season, is not an ending but a time to celebrate the yield brought forth from work and care and the simple passage of time. Harvest is the opposite of barren in my thesaurus.

The harvest season is a time in a woman's life when she can reap the benefits of how far she has come and gather the wisdom and self-knowledge that have matured in her first 50 years. This bounty will nourish the rest of her life. So you can look upon the findings in this book as a sort of farmer's market for the feminine—organic, maybe a bit raw for some, but, I sincerely hope, nourishing food for thought.

CHAPTER 1:

Getting Here Was Only Was Only Half the Fun

One day this question just popped into my head: "When the biological imperative to reproduce is gone, what is a woman's role in society? What is a woman to do when her 'natural' purpose is outlived?"

I suppose that, in asking this question, I made several assumptions. I assumed that the reproductive imperative was part of the female nature, hardwired in all women. I acknowledged that it is activated in some and dormant in others, but still the imperative is part of all women's biological makeup.

For more insight into biology, I looked to the animal kingdom for answers. I discovered that the timing of menopause in the human life-span can be compared to that found in baboons and lions. This is confirmed by research conducted by the University of Minnesota ecologist Craig Packer. I was pleased by this association, as I consider lions and baboons worthy biological soul mates; I was relieved not to be scientifically validated by hyenas or jackals.

*As human life expectancy advances,
our daughters and granddaughters may live as
many years after menopause as they do before.*

.

The female human, lion, and baboon were originally designed to live only as long as it took the last round of offspring to survive independently. This is approximately one year for lions, two years for baboons, and ten years for humans. But in modern times, human life expectancy has expanded much more than life expectancy in the rest of the animal kingdom, and the human female in most cultures far outlives that original design. In *Healthy Transitions: A Woman's Guide to Perimenopause, Menopause & Beyond*, Neil Shulman, M.D., and Edmund S. Kim, M.D., write that the average age of menopause has long been around 51, so in the early 1900s "many women died before they completely went through menopause. In the early 1900s menopause was potentially a signal that a woman's life was close to the end. . . . Now women live into their 80s and beyond. A woman born today can expect to live over a third of her life after she goes through menopause." As life expectancy rapidly advances, it is reasonable to expect that our daughters and granddaughters may live as many years after menopause as they do before.

Occasionally a lioness or a female baboon will also outlive the one- or two-year milestone. When this happens and the female is left with no offspring of her own who require her immediate attention, there is evidence that she takes on a new role in the pride or band as a community caregiver. These animal seniors become wise old aunties of sorts who pick up the chores that the more role-oriented youth don't have time for, caring for orphans, cleaning up the feeding grounds, and picking out the nits for the mateless. In a world that revolves around hunting and eating, surviving predators and disease, and breeding to keep the race viable, these "aunty" chores are quite important.

So what of the female human? What is her role in these years past the span of her original design?

THE VIEW FROM UP HERE

My mother lived to be 92. It was her passing, in part, that stimulated this exploration of a woman's life at 50+. All of a sudden I felt pushed off the bench and onto the field, out of the wings onto the stage. "Okay, here I am fully in the game, no longer the understudy. But wait a minute—what position am I playing, what is my role? My kids are grown, my biological work is done, but obviously I am still supposed to contribute or I would not be center stage." There is irony in losing your mother when you are menopausal—no longer a daughter and no longer able to become a mother. Once again the universe schedules life in a way that tosses us brilliantly into first panic, then renewal.

In a larger sense, I believe the problem we face in aging is that we are not prepared to live longer. The physical evolution of our species has surpassed the plans we have made. If you listen closely, when this realization hits you, you will actually hear the gods—yours, mine, everyone's—laughing, ever so subtly, in the background.

We have used science and knowledge to improve our health, and with this newly minted vigor we have climbed exponentially up the life-expectancy chart. We have managed to scale the highest peaks in history, and now, as we rest and lean back on the chart line, we look out over the graph paper and discover the vast empty space of an ever-expanding future.

*The problem we face in aging is that we are
not prepared to live longer.
The evolution of our species has surpassed
the plans we have made.*

Oops . . . all that climbing and here we are facing that nasty unknown stuff again. Do not despair. Yes, the air is a little thinner up here (and we are certainly not thinner)—but we are not alone. Women 50 and over are a glut on the market, though that's a rather less than positive way to describe the size of our age and gender cohort. And we are not only a force of many. Today's postmenopausal female also has more wealth, health, and power than ever before.

Quite a presence, don't you think? I cannot help but wonder what the impact would be if we applied our numbers and our strength to live fully in this time. What could we learn? What could the world learn? It is these questions that led me to the Women of the Harvest.

THE ONLY WAY OUT IS THROUGH

The experience of unavoidable and irreversible change within our bodies can cause a certain amount of discomfort.

Wasn't *discomfort* the euphemism they used in prenatal classes to describe the physical sensations you were going to experience in the *transition* stage of labor?

My prenatal coach defined transition as the point when the laboring woman wants to say, "Okay, I've had enough now. I'm going home. I'll just leave my uterus here on the table. You can carry on without me." It seems that in midlife we get the urge to repeat this escape. But, as in labor, once the process has started, there is no door that leads out—only one that leads through.

Transition is an excellent word to describe the stage in a woman's life that begins around menopause. It is when she first begins to experience the signs of change. Many of these changes will not occur until years after menopause, but she begins to see their inevitability.

Faced with a new horizon to inhabit, finding yourself unprepared and without a defined role, it is understandable that you might turn back to a familiar past. The days and ways of your youth were comfortable; you knew who you were then and what you needed to do and be. Well, perhaps you did not know those things when you were actually living those days, but now that they've been lived and you look back, it seems you knew. Surely you knew. Right?

A little surgery, a new outfit—a bit too short but what the heck, you still have the legs—and there: you are that again, your very own past. Only one problem—you are not that again. This is your life, and it progresses and evolves. You cannot ever be that again.

THE NEXT, BEST HALF

When menopause occurs and the physical and psychological imperatives of the female reproductive system fall away, a new frontier opens for women. At this time in history, that frontier stretches farther out on the horizon than ever before. It is a full season, not a semi-season like Indian summer or the February blahs. This is a rich time in a woman's life because we come to these days ripened by the journey that got us here and clear about the fact that we are still learning and that self-knowledge is a lifetime pursuit.

Joyful living comes from the ability to utilize the energy that is inherent in each stage of life. Menopause and post-menopause, as stages of the female life, contain their own unique and powerful energies. Margaret Mead called this energy "zest." Anne Morrow Lindbergh's metaphor in *Gift from the Sea* was the Argonauta, or paper nautilus—the symbol of a stage of life that evolves from the maturation in the years which preceded it. The female Argonauta holds what appears to be her shell in her arms while her eggs mature. Then, after the eggs hatch, she and the young are released into the sea to start the next stage of their lives.

Gift from the Sea is a must-read for women in transition. This wise and graceful book, which celebrated its fiftieth birthday a few years ago, Lindbergh writes that many people "never climb above the plateau of 40-to-50. The signs that presage growth . . . are interpreted falsely as signs of decay." She goes on: "Because of the false assumption that [middle age] is a period of decline, one interprets these life signs, paradoxically, as signs of approaching death. Instead of facing them, one runs away." Lindbergh describes this new stage of growth, from which people run, as a new stage of living "when, having shed many of the physical struggles, the worldly ambitions, the material encumbrances of active life, one might be free to fulfill the neglected side of one's self. One might be free for growth of mind, heart and talent; free at last for spiritual growth."

We come to these days ripened by the journey that got us here and clear about the fact that we are still learning.

One Woman of the Harvest told me, reflecting on the obsession to stay young, "It is sad to age in fear of the absence of something you don't have anymore, like youth." But in Western society particularly, the prevalent image of aging is one of loss. Now, the Women of the Harvest are not exempt from the natural processes of age. They endure their own physical decline, an inescapable reality. They suffer the struggles and loss of loved ones. They have serious financial concerns that keep them working 50 hours a week well into their 70s. It is not that life presents a different reality for those who have embraced their harvest. It is their *attitude* toward our shared reality that distinguishes them.

Losses are inevitable, because they are physical realities for this age group. But focus on what is lost and it is the losses that become your experience of life after 50. Focus on what is found and your experience will be life's continuing gifts.

Yes, aging is a time for loss, but what you may discover is that less can be more.

Ask yourself this simple question:
What do I know now that I did not know before,
and what can I do with that knowledge to make
this the next, best half of my life?

The new horizon of 50+ lies ahead. You did not invite it. It is not inviting you, at least not in a way that suggests you could, if you wished, politely decline. You can turn your back and try to capture youth once more. You can spend a lot of time and effort there, and you can even gain a little ground on that slippery slope—science is amazing. At the other extreme, you can fold your cards, not turn away completely, but just sit still: chair pushed slightly back from the table, hands in your lap, watching others play quietly, all the time just waiting for the end.

Or you can step forward, women 50+, and place those well-worn, perhaps pedicured, maybe callused feet onto new terrain, the fields of the harvest. Step forward and ask yourself this simple question: *What do I know now that I did not know before, and what can I do with that knowledge to make this the next, best half of my life?*

CRONE ROSES

I have become obsessed with roses in full bloom. You know, the loud, heavy-laden ones that speak to you when you walk past: "Hey, you, over here, look!" They are not shyly peeping out like new buds or stretching their length like slim youth on the beach. The roses I love are big. They are splayed open with petals curled at the edges because they have been beaten and blown by their time in the sun and wind.

These are what I call Crone Roses. I use the word crone not with the harsh and ugly connotations it's come to have, but in its original sense—the way mythologist Joseph Campbell used it in The Hero with a Thousand Faces—as the archetype of the wise woman whose mature experience enriches all around her. I think the crone is a wonderful symbol for the wisdom in an older woman, and I hope we can restore the term it to its former glory.

These roses rest slightly bent on their cane stems, too heavy for the old support system to handle now. Their scent alone is a weight, a heavy, intoxicating mixture of the sun-soaked days of the past and a life lived long. These old beauties are elegance, not the refined elegance of things that are highly stylized and overly proper but the elegance that is earned by time and passion, and each becomes a unique gift to your garden.

Can you imagine your garden with just the younger blooms, without the contrast of the older ones?

What do you think the buds learn from the full-bloom beauties at night when we go indoors and leave them alone under the stars?

Go out into your garden and find a Crone Rose, and then clip a younger rose too. Take them both inside and set them side by side in a vase. What do you see?

When does different become better or worse? When we look through the veil of judgment. This veil filters our senses and steals pure sight, sound, or taste, replacing it with other people's messages and our personal fears.

If you could enjoy the older rose without that annoying little voice in your head that tells you it is fading, it has seen better days . . . then you could truly experience its beauty.

Hmmm . . . what if you could look in the mirror, or at your mother, without that little voice? What would you see?

For Your Reflection

Think about a change you have undergone in your own life, whether it's passing 50 or some other transition. What did you lose in the process? What did you find?

Have you tried to recapture an earlier stage of your life—for example, by having cosmetic surgery or dressing a certain way? How successful have your efforts been?

Imagine that you are looking out at the long horizon of your life. What do you see?

CHAPTER 2:

Mirror, Mirror on the Wall . . . Can You Still See Me at All?

I got an e-mail advertisement today. The subject line popped off the screen: "Get Noticed Again." Yes, my spam filter had worked and this ad was in the junk box, but I was so intrigued by this headline that I opened it. It was an ad for face cream!

What an interesting concept. I am currently unnoticeable because of the lines on my face, and if I remove those lines I will be noticeable once more. When did I become unnoticeable, I ask myself?

Often when life sets a tough task in front of us, it helps us to embrace the challenge by changing the environment we live in so that our choice of action becomes unavoidable. Just as I began to think about interviewing women about their experience of life 50+, I started to notice a trend. When I talked with female friends and associates, the same word kept coming up over and over again.

"Get Noticed Again,"
the ad said.
When did I become unnoticeable?

Women 50+ from a variety of social, political, and geographical cultures were using the same word to describe how they felt in their many roles: *invisible*. They told me that for the first time in their lives, they felt unheard in the workplace, in social situations, and in their communities.

These are skilled, experienced, and wise women. Surely what they have to say is valuable—but how can they share it if they are unheard?

I was already somewhat committed to exploring the post-50 years, but when this "invisible" phenomenon came up I was hooked and, given the subject matter, I guess we need to complete the analogy—hooked like a salmon on her way upstream.

I realized that the urge to explore and celebrate the richness of these years in a woman's life was not exactly going to be going with the flow . . . but that never stopped a salmon.

NOW YOU SEE ME, NOW YOU DON'T

In aging, the pursuit of youth is mostly about the visible—the face and the body—because this is the first place we notice the change happening. (Hence the e-mails about face cream.)

Many of us did not pay much attention to that same body when we were younger. I think perhaps we got it backwards. In youth we invested in our minds and in the accumulation of our things, often leaving the thriving body to take care of itself. But once the body starts to give off signals that it really can't manage on its own anymore, we are in there working to shore up the walls of the fortress that binds us.

U.S. health and personal-care stores generated over $200 billion in sales in 2007, with Americans spending over $30 billion on cosmetics and beauty supplies and services, according to the U.S. Census Bureau. That's $30 billion, just in the U.S, spent each year on products and services that promise to reverse or at least retard the inevitable deterioration of the body—$30 billion all spent to turn amber back into wood, a diamond back into sand. Get it? In nature we acknowledge that aging creates value. But when it comes to our personal aging we seem to have rejected that premise. We discount the span of our lives and the breadth of our being and instead exert all this effort to recapture a fleeting time in the life history of the body alone.

In some ways I envy those inanimate objects, wood and sand—they are blessed to exist without a nagging ego to tell them that they are losing what they had, they have no idea what their future selves will look like, on and on. We sorry humans do have that voice to contend with, but in a delightful irony, we cherish the aged in nature. We even spend big money to wind our own aged forms in gold and silver to de-emphasize our own evolution.

The U.S. cosmetics and beauty services industry generates $30 billion in business annually— $30 billion all spent to turn amber back into wood, a diamond back into sand.

One of the women I interviewed posed an interesting question. She noted that women "generally feel good when they know they look good," and then she asked, "Is this a biological reaction or a psychological reaction?"

I don't know the right answer to this question, but I think it does offer an opportunity to poke our heads below the surface of our beliefs about ourselves. Sometimes when we discover the root of a personal belief, we also discover it is tying us down to something that really does not serve us anymore, and then whew . . . we can let it go.

It's not difficult to see the argument for biology: we need to be attractive in order to attract a mate and reproduce. Sorry, of course I know it has all evolved to a much higher level in modern society, but somewhere deep in our DNA, attractiveness is still a matter of survival. Psychologically, it's not so different; the connection between perceived attractiveness and emotional well-being is often related to biologically rooted self-esteem. When you are "breed-worthy," you feel better about yourself and the world, and so your world, at least, is all in order. When you look at it this way you realize that this concern for your appearance is not some vain obsession; quite the opposite. This link between feeling good and looking good can also be programmed in through the messages we received while growing up and continue to receive from the media. So in the end I do not think that we can assign full credit (or blame) to either biology or psychology. The fact is that many women feel better when they think they look better, and feeling better means more confident, braver, more capable. This is a common feminine reality, perhaps arising where biology and psychology meet.

The biology of our gender is ever-present. It may be well dressed, discreetly covered, and buried deep beneath our educated minds and evolved social mores, but the sex hormone is active in every social interaction our species conducts. I think this biological reality is the seed of the power conflicts and insecurities that often play out in the workplace and social settings—as well as the key to the way we mysteriously drop out of sight at 50+.

When menopause occurs, our biology changes; the instinctual imperative to reproduce diminishes and then completely disappears. The biological changes manifest changes in our relationships as well, because unconsciously the world around us notes that something is not as it used to be. Men and younger women are less tacitly aware of us. Their unconscious attraction is diminished or their competitive guard goes down, so we slip off their screens. We become, in a word, invisible. And our invisibility is just the environment's reaction to the reduction in sex-hormone production that occurs after menopause.

DON'T FIGHT YOUR POWER

Gail Sheehy said in *New Passages*, "Women don't have to apologize for wanting power after they've been sex objects."

But invisibility over 50 can be rooted much earlier in life. In the workplace, many women still do not walk comfortably in the shoes of leadership. They struggle with how to bring feminine power to their leadership roles even though they experience the strength of their gender in their personal lives. They ask themselves and their mentors: What is female power? Does it exist distinct from male power?

Some women who cannot find the feminine way emulate the power of men. They watch the men who have succeeded—still, unfortunately, often the majority in the roles these women aspire to—and they study how they operate: their leadership style, the way they communicate, the way they make decisions, the values they seem to be guided by. Then these aspiring women try to copy their male role models.

But women are different from men. We think, communicate, act differently. Not better, just differently. In trying to act just like the men, we deny ourselves important benefits. A perfect workplace—well, maybe a utopian workplace—would encourage the differences and so produce the ultimate result from a mix of male and female thinking. Those women who "copy" the men often succeed in the short run, but put themselves at risk later in life because rather than investing in their own sense of self they are renting space in someone else's. They will not benefit from the interest that accrues when a woman invests in developing her own unique feminine brain-power and perspective. These women who have lived less authentically will be most affected by their perceived invisibility. As their femininity is tested, seemingly diminished by aging, they will seek to fall back on something, their adopted maleness, that was a chimera all along.

Some women in leadership roles think they need to emulate the power of men. But they put themselves at risk, because rather than investing in their own sense of self they are renting space in someone else's.

Sung-Joo Kim, chairperson and CEO of the fashion and retail company Sungjoo Group/MCM Group, is one of the most celebrated businesswomen in Asia. The Asian culture magnified the challenges of female leadership for Sung-Joo, but she found a way through it to her own authentic form of power—her own highly visible wisdom harvest. Speaking at a Women's Leadership Exchange conference in Long Beach, California, she urged women "to stop struggling with their femininity and embrace it as their unique strength." In other words, find your strengths—not your weaknesses—for leadership and life in that which is feminine, because that is what you are.

The Women of the Harvest have survived the event of imposed invisibility, and they have done so by laying down their arms in the fight against themselves. These women, our heroines, know that through all the battles and trials of life, whether we nurture it or abuse it, our femininity does not diminish. It remains waiting to be embraced, understood, and finally used to our advantage.

THE BEAUTY OF PRESENCE

In *A Walk on the Beach*, Joan Anderson quotes her mentor Joan Erikson, the wife and collaborator of pioneering psychologist Erik Erikson. On her 94th birthday, Ms. Erikson said: "Our bodies wear out, our thoughts come more slowly. But our life cycles are our most creative effort. We can't ever not be in them, right? The struggle is to try and obtain a sense of participation in your life the whole way through."

There is a beauty available to our lives that has been grossly undervalued, not because it lacks power—far from it—but because it is underexplored and undefined.

I believe that when we ignore the natural cycle of life and attempt to remake a previous stage, we cheat ourselves out of the creativity that is available to us in the act of participating in the stage we're in. "No thanks, really, I'll sit this one out on the sidelines of my *former* life." When we take this attitude, we do become invisible, because we simply aren't present. We fail to show up for our own lives.

Perhaps this invisibility is the universe urging us to rediscover ourselves and to redefine our concept of what we are by consciously integrating the lessons that life has given us so far. Then, as we see ourselves afresh, we will be seen by others in a different way too. There is a beauty available to our lives that has been grossly undervalued, not because it is subtle or retiring, not because it fails to attract and fascinate, not even because it lacks power—far from it—but because it is underexplored and undefined. We live in a society that values the things we can define and evaluate, and we ignore and fear the unknown. So great is our fear that we would lose an entire season from our lives rather than embrace something we cannot quickly understand. The last stage of life, for many, is a steep slide into the unknown, and so we leave it unexplored, lest we uncover some truth we don't want to see or some fact we can not control . . . like our mortality, perhaps?

Many women struggle with their personal relationship to beauty for most of their lives. Enough, ladies! If you will explore the changing and the unknown and acknowledge the new, you can finally get comfortable with what beauty means to you. Then you will clearly see when you are in the presence of great beauty—others' and your own.

REMEMBER THE CRONE ROSE?

The beauty of the ripe rose is in the grace with which it lays open its core exposing the broadened surface of the petals. A woman in fullest bloom stands in vulnerability but not in fear. The rose and the woman both offer one final radiant expression of life . . . because what can you steal from one who offers you everything?

For Your Reflection

Have you ever felt invisible—in the workplace, in a social situation, or in your community? What were the circumstances? How did you respond?

If you are in a leadership role—for example, in your work—where does your power come from?

Ask yourself: are you sitting on the sidelines of your life? Or are you showing up for your life right now?

CHAPTER 3:

Who Are These Women?

If you are finding any wisdom in these pages, it is because you are hearing the voices of the Women of the Harvest—women who have not run from aging but do not simply wait for its inevitable passage either.

I remember my first encounters with such women vividly. I was small, maybe only four or five years old. These women were intriguing like a storybook. They were a little scary, too—that would have been my word at four, but now it might be "intimidating." They seemed happy and mischievous but often said things that seemed to make other adults un-comfortable. When this tension between them and the other adults hung in the air, they would often turn and look at me as if we shared a secret. A secret between this old woman who had lived and seen and learned so much and this small child who did not yet know what she did not know. Their kisses were usually wet because their lips were no longer firm and there was no collagen in those days. Most of all I remember their eyes. I thought I could play in their eyes forever!

I know now that part of my attraction to these wonderful, sparkling older women was because they had stepped up to Joan Erikson's challenge. They were fully participating in life—how engaging is *that?*

In *A Walk on the Beach*, Joan Anderson succinctly describes why people were drawn to the 94-year-old Erikson: "everyone is wishing to draw more nourishment from her naughty twinkle, upbeat intonation, and playfulness."

So it was easy to find the Women of the Harvest. I just looked for that twinkle.

I described the women I sought simply: older women with a light in their eyes. At first I thought this was just my private description of what I saw in remarkable older women, and I anticipated that it might be met with blank stares. But it turned out everyone knew what I meant, because the beauty of these women engages anyone who is fortunate enough to encounter it.

When I called one nursing home, the director said, "Yes, I know someone here like that, but I warn you, she is not the easiest woman to get along with."

Well, of course not! She is not the easiest and her life has not been the easiest, but that is exactly the point. She still shines and we need to know why—now.

THE SHINING MOMENT

It seemed as if everyone knew someone I should speak to, and I was invited into a world that was deeper and richer than I could ever have anticipated. With amazing openness and grace, women told me their stories, shared their intimate perspectives on the roles they played in life after 50, and described the forces that drive them as they age.

Some of the women I interviewed are compulsively active, assertive, and outgoing, but some are quiet and work in more subtle ways. Their insight, vision, and perspective on life sets them apart, but it may not always show in their actions. Sometimes you know a Woman of the Harvest only by her unique sense of presence and the way it allows her to receive what life brings each day.

Is this the ultimate maturity—to bear the moment of now, to stand courageously to receive what life delivers each day? Ironically, it appears to be almost the opposite of what we define as maturity. It is a childlike innocence, but an innocence that comes *with* knowledge, not *before* knowledge. One woman told me, "My sense of wonder comes from being focused on the present moment, not knowing what is coming next and not caring."

Some of the women I interviewed are compulsively active, assertive, and outgoing, but some are quiet and work in much more subtle ways. It is their perspective on life that sets them apart.

Another said, "This light which shines comes from a deep sense of safety, an innocent knowing that you are safe. You receive the world with the openness of a trusting child, secure in yourself and knowing there is nothing to truly harm you."

This twinkle in the eyes of the Woman of the Harvest is a cosmetic to die for!

Using the word twinkle to describe it makes it sound small and demure, doesn't it? But think again. Stars, which are really just gargantuan raging masses of fire—they twinkle, don't they? Perhaps some women have this light from birth, but it doesn't shine as strongly in the fresh face of youth. It takes the furrows of time and the weathering of life to really set it off.

I believe that the twinkle is the light of a life focused on this very moment, not diffused over the past and the future. Think about what happens when the beam from a lighthouse circles around and hits you right in the face. How much brighter is that than the same wattage diffused in the opposite direction?

So how do we get ourselves some twinkle? I don't think we can get it, but it can get us. It comes as a gift—and if it is the logical consequence of any characteristic, anything that we could look for as a clue, that is acceptance. In the words of one woman I spoke to, "In life you are presented with choices but you do not control the options." The wonder of accepting the unknown and uncontrollable in your life—that's what ignites the spark in the eyes. Have you ever met someone and later said you felt "seen" by her? The seeing is the light her eyes cast on you.

*I believe that the twinkle
in these women's eyes is the light of a life focused
on this very moment. Think about what happens
when the beam from a lighthouse circles around
and hits you right in the face.*

¡YO HABLO ESPAÑOL OLÉ!

In youth we look forward. Our next birthday cannot come fast enough, and we are full of dreams and plans that fill the endless distance to the horizon. It is as if for the first 30 or 40 years of our life we equate aging with increasing freedom and so we want to bring on the advancing years as quickly as possible. As teenagers we dream of being out on óur own and making our own decisions. When we are 25 or 35 we dream of the fine future we are building for ourselves and those around us and the freedom to live as we please that the work we do today will earn for our future, promotions, respect, summer vacations and college for our kids.

In midlife, we turn our gaze backwards. I am not sure why we turn from the future to the past. I think in part we are motivated by the changing landscape we see ahead. In midlife, the horizon that stretches before us is suddenly frightening. When our parents have passed and changes in our health have nudged the reality of our own mortality into view, that horizon shifts. Once it was the place where all our dreams would come true; now it's an unknown space that eventually leads to the edge of the world as we know it.

The Women of the Harvest are too busy for the past and the future. They have work to do. Anyway, they know that the past cannot be changed and the future cannot be predicted. They are at peace with this. They have not given up the dream of a better future for themselves, their families, and the planet, but they know that the past and the future are not places of action, and so they bring their energy for those dreams to the present moment.

Once the horizon was the place where all our dreams would come true; now it's an unknown space that eventually leads to the edge of the world as we know it.

They work and live fully engaged in what is here now. They have lived their past and left it there. They do not carry it with them packed in guilty or prideful luggage. They are interested in the future, but their faith in what it will bring is fed by the actions they take today, not by passive worries or dreams. You could say they possess an elegance that's not timeless, but timely.

Look at it this way. If you are 65 today, in 20 years you will be 85. Let's say you have always dreamed of being fluent in a foreign language. If you start studying Spanish today, on your 85th birthday you could say, *¡yo hablo español olé!* Or you could decide it's too late. Either way, in 20 years you will be 85, *hablando español o sin hablar español* (speaking Spanish or not).

When we live today blinded by concerns about tomorrow or regrets about yesterday, we create the self-fulfilling prophecy of the age of decline. Focusing on the past or future drains our energy. Focusing on the present can energize us because we feel the impact of our actions. The energy available to us 50+ has changed, not in quality and I don't even want to say in quantity but in some evaluative way after 50 life's energy is changed. It is changed in the way we perceive it. After 50 we know that our energy is a limited resource, not the limitless one we thought we had in our youth. We start to feel it in a deeper, more concentrated way. So it is natural that we begin to think about how to use that energy more efficiently and effectively. Worry and fear use energy, but they never fixed anything. However, energy applied to action today could improve tomorrow.

If you start studying Spanish today, on your 85th birthday you could say, ¡yo hablo español olé! Or you could decide it's too late. In 20 years you will be 85, either way.

Do you ever find yourself wondering what folks will say about you when you are gone? Come on, admit it—you do sometimes, don't you? It's not really as morbid as you think. It is a natural thing to do after being at a funeral or reading the obituaries in the paper. We are drawn to think about how people will describe us at the end of our lives. I think the real question is: what do we want to say about ourselves today?

One of the things that amazed me was the value my interviewees found in the process of answering the questions I posed. It seems that not all Women of the Harvest know how remarkable they are. This is the ultimate unconscious competence!

What is "unconscious competence"? It's a term used in organizational development to describe employees who know a great deal and are highly effective without being aware of it. With awareness comes even greater competence and even better performance. It is not a use-it-or-lose-it scenario, but using it knowingly will definitely double the impact. In the terminology of this book, we would call that a bumper crop!

I have shared what I learned from the Women of the Harvest to encourage other women to bring their unconscious competence into full awareness—to use all they know, do all they can do, and celebrate this stage of the female life as it has never been celebrated before. It's my hope that you will join in this celebration.

> *We are drawn to think about how people will describe us at the end of our lives. I think the real question is: what do we want to say about ourselves today?*

Time is going to pass. If you are 50 now, in 40 years you will be 90. The question is, will you find your moment of fullness and live out those 40 years there?

NATURE'S PERFECT DESIGN—YOU

As we begin to look at the characteristics of the Women of the Harvest, it becomes apparent that the human female species is a perfect design of nature. In the world of plants, as the flower withers, the seedpod develops and so the next generation is assured—and in perennials that process will repeat itself as a perfect natural function each year. The human female is a perennial of sorts. She may experience multiple periods of fertility and even a period of fertility postmenopause that brings forth, not offspring, but a new generation of thought and purpose. Postmenopausal fertility blossoms when a woman reframes her outlook on aging, taking the focus off the losses and discovering the gifts.

The human female is a perennial of sorts. She may experience multiple periods of fertility and even a period of fertility postmenopause that brings forth, not offspring, but a new generation of thought and purpose.

As the flower of femininity, the body, starts to decline, we develop new mental and psychological strengths, and these become the resources with which we can craft our legacy. "Wait, you say, I am not at the legacy stage yet—I am still actively growing and contributing." That is exactly the point. The legacy you will leave, much later in life, is being crafted every day along the way. When age taps you on the shoulder it is a timely reminder to stop and reflect, with the perspective of your accumulated years, on what your future legacy may be. Then you continue, bringing all the gifts of your reflection, to the work and the living you are engaged in and so to your eventual legacy. A legacy is not something that suddenly materializes when you retire; it grows in every action you take along the way. We need to reflect at each stage of our lives, because as we live and experience, part of what changes is our fundamental outlook on life.

And this is an enormous change. When our outlook changes, so does the way we experience everything, because outlook is the receptor of experience. Think clean windows versus dirty windows!

The Women of the Harvest, women who embrace aging in all its aspects, do not waste much time mourning the decline of the physical. Physical changes are noted and checked off, and then they move on to the more important and exciting developments, many of which I will shortly present for your consideration.

These women are not exempt from the physical and psychological realities of the advancing years. They just receive them differently. For them, the loss of one thing does not leave a gap—it creates a space in which a new reality seeds and grows.

I suppose you could say that these women have faith in their perfection—the perfection of their design—and they have faith in the designer. The female human is not the product of a modern assembly line, designed for obsolescence long before its utility is over. We have a contribution to make—it is *not* over yet!

I do not think the outlook of The Women of the Harvest is new. I believe it has been available to us since the beginning of time. But only some of us have manifested it; the rest of us resist.

> *We have a contribution to make—*
> *it is not over yet!*

HAVE FAITH IN YOUR BRAIN

Why do we keep that fight up, the fight against our own nature? Have we lost faith in our original design—or have we lost the ability to make it work in the world, so that we have to put our energy into rejecting it until we find a new way to be what we were originally designed to be?

Why do we keep up the fight against our own nature?
Have we lost faith in our original design—or have we
lost the ability to make it work in the world?

Louann Brizendine, a neuropsychiatrist at the University of California–San Francisco and author of *The Female Brain*, provides some fascinating facts that may help us begin accepting ourselves. The key to a happier and more peaceful life, we know, is in that clarity and acceptance.

Dr. Brizendine describes how the female brain actually differs from the male brain—in structure and therefore in function—and how it was all perfectly designed to protect and develop the species. Mother Nature knew exactly what she was doing.

Simply put, the part of the female brain called the anterior cingulate cortex—as Dr. Brizendine puts it, "the worry-wort center"—is larger in women than in men.

Among other things, this area of the female brain supports an enhanced ability to read what others are thinking or feeling. "Developmental psychologists believe that the female brain's extreme ability to connect through reading faces, interpreting tones of voice, and registering nuances of emotion are traits that were selected evolutionarily from the time of the Stone Age," she writes. "These traits make it possible for the female brain to pick up cues from nonverbal infants and anticipate their needs." In other words, women have extra radar to help them meet the needs of the infants they must protect and nurture.

Not only is this good for mothering, it can give us amazing intuitive powers that apply in other situations. But this hypersensitivity to others can be problematic. The anterior cingulate cortex "is a critical area for anticipating, judging, controlling, and integrating negative emotions," Dr. Brizendine goes on to say. Our judging can turn on ourselves and morph into worried self-doubt in response to the normal biological need to maintain physical attractiveness and social connection.

So while our "super sensitivity" makes us great moms, partners, and leaders, it can also be the source of a critical inner voice that evaluates our performance.

Women are built with extra radar to help them meet the needs of the infants they must nurture. But our hypersensitivity to others can turn on us and morph into worried self-doubt.

So how do the Women of the Harvest overcome this difficult side of themselves?

One woman I interviewed explains very well how she's shifted her hardwired self-criticism: "In my youth I tended to focus more on what I perceived as my negative characteristics. I realize now that what I was really trying to do was gain approval from others. I thought 'fixing' me would get me the approval I craved. I still see aspects of my character that I don't like, but I don't worry about them as much, because, quite frankly, I don't care what people think of me nearly as much as I used to. This leaves a lot more time in my life to really enjoy the parts of me I like."

The Women of the Harvest have come to live at peace with their natural female tendencies, including their fine-tuned emotional radar. That does not mean you have to always like all these wonderful "blessings of the gender." Does anyone really *like* a menstrual period? No, but you have to admit it serves a purpose. When you stop wasting energy on resistance, you can simply see it as what it is: a function that serves us well overall but is less convenient in some circumstances than in others. On the positive side, your larger and more influential anterior cingulate cortex is also the source of your unique feminine strengths— exactly the qualities Sung-Joo Kim has harvested into a

77

multi-million-dollar company, not to mention considerable peace and grace. Have faith in what you are, ladies, it is well designed and it works.

CONFIDENCE, TRUTH, AND THE UNWRAPPING OF US

You read the most amazing wisdom on the Internet. I found this on a blog recently: "Women give themselves away to functions, husbands, children, and work." I think this quote speaks to what the Women of the Harvest uncover as they begin the work of reaping *their* crop of wisdom. They not only discover a new season in their lives, they discover *themselves*, long ago dropped on the field of responsibility and service to others.

Each Women of the Harvest has unwrapped a most amazing package. Maybe she found this package under a cabbage leaf . . . after all, we're working with a farming metaphor here. Or maybe her harvest package is a brightly decorated box painted cherry red and tied up with a designer bow. It is, however, a Pandora's Box, because once it is opened its contents can never be hidden again. As the ribbon comes loose and the paper falls away, the lid slides off—and out come your confidence, your self-esteem, and the truth of your voice. When you breathe life into these gifts by recognizing them for what they are—even for a moment—they expand like a flowering tea bud. There is no way they are going to fit back in that box, and there is no way you would want to put them back in that box.

I would change that blog statement only slightly. I would say, "Women give themselves to functions, husbands, children, and work," not give themselves away. Giving is done gladly, with love and joy and dedication. *Given away* sounds a bit like cast to the wind, even wasted, and I do not believe that the stage in a woman's life that builds a family or career or community is wasted in any way.

Remember, real beauty lies in a full and varied garden. Maybe I sounded a little dismissive of the new-bloomed rose a few chapters back, but I know that this life is about both the new bud and the full bloom. It is about the opposites we love to love and love to hate, because all of them have their unique aspect to celebrate.

Many years ago I learned a vital lesson about change: Honor the past and build on it. We need not ever dismiss or diminish yesterday to honor and celebrate today.

A ROOM CALLED YOU

Think of the countless times you have tried to create your own
space, physically or metaphorically, in your life—just a tiny little
area that is yours. Was it your first tree house or the fort under
your bed? Later a chair in your shared bedroom? Eventually, if
you were really lucky, your space grew up into a study or your
very own office?

Or maybe it is just a space in your head, a moment of
awareness.

What makes this room your own, and why do you seek it
your whole life?

There is magic in these spaces and that magic defines a
room as "yours." When you shut the doors, real or imagined, to
your room, another door within the room opens and there is a
glimpse into infinity that reminds you that no matter what you
were when you entered this space, within this space you embody
endless potential.

In this room of yours, you are safe, and what is conceived
in this space is born of the confidence and self-knowledge that
safety allows. In this room, risk is magically morphed into
adventure. In this room, the mirrors show one perfect face, one

perfect body, because they hold your image not in glass but in the reflection of self-respect.

Very selectively you might invite someone else into this space . . . a child curled in your lap for a minute or a spouse offering a cup of tea. They leave a little discombobulated. "That was nice," they think to themselves as they wander off, not quite sure where they have been but knowing it felt good.

What if your 50th birthday is the doorway into this room? What if, from that day on, you live in your room, a room of your own, a room called you. No more stolen moments—this space is this season of your life.

I can see you now, dressed to kill, grinning ear to ear, sashaying your way up to those 50 birthday candles with a light in your eyes, ready to take possession of your room. "I am here," you say. "I have arrived."

Many years ago I learned a vital lesson about change and made it the cornerstone of my work on this topic: honor the past and build on it. If you discredit what has gone before to establish the new order, you set your new foundation on shaky ground. You will dishearten the people you want to work alongside you in the new order; you will rob them of the richness of their experience and all they have ever learned. We need not ever dismiss or diminish yesterday to honor and celebrate today.

THE ROAD TO YOU

Margaret Trudeau, who underwent a very public separation and divorce from Canadian prime minister Pierre Trudeau in the midst of his tenure, has had more than her fair share of challenges in life. At 60, she told Toronto's *Globe and Mail* that she finds great value in her advancing age. "Freedom! I smile at the memories, wince and wink for the bad ones, and know that I have lived."

So what do we do with our bad memories, our regrets? Got any? I have a few—well, actually, quite a list—but I learned this from the Women of the Harvest: I must face an event that I regret honestly, even to the point of seeing it as something I wish with all my heart I had done differently.

Then, with grace, I can find a place for it to sit so that it does not block my view of life today. When I find that place, just like a puzzle piece, the regret becomes integrated and part of the whole. It completes the person I am today.

The past may have been a rough road, but it was your road. Self-knowledge is about knowing all of yourself and living today better for knowing. The last breath you took brought you to this moment and this breath takes you to the next and you can't just store the good breaths to keep the lungs going. You must breathe each moment of each day, even if sometimes the air is not very pure.

I must face an event that I regret honestly, even to the point of seeing it as something I wish with all my heart I had done differently.

The horizon that opens up for women 50+ is a time horizon. That is what it offers, time, and that is where your road leads you now. Earlier in life you gladly focused on the lives and pursuits of others; now you have time to discover yourself. You will be amazed, I promise.

I am pretty sure that the expression "finding myself" was coined in the '60s by, you guessed it, the Boomer generation. I remember telling my mother that I had to hitchhike around Europe to "find myself." She did not like this idea. "Your sisters found themselves in North America. Why do you have to go to Europe?"

It looks like we are still at it, finding ourselves. But if you think this is another boomer-aged exercise in self-absorption, take a look at what we've turned up.

When I asked the Women of the Harvest what surprises they found in their personal inventory at this stage of life, they answered, smiling:

- Resilience
- Forgiveness
- Confidence
- Completeness
- Truth
- Risk
- Fullness
- Compassion
- Leadership
- Solitude
- Wisdom
- Intuition
- Passion

- **Vulnerability**
- **Skill**
- **Talent**
- **Success**
- **Voice**
- **Peace**

This list is the harvest of self-knowledge—and it's only a partial list at that.

What and who will it nourish?

For Your Reflection

Do you know an older woman with that certain light in her eyes? Where do you think she gets it?

How do you deal with bad memories, or with regrets, when you look back at the rough spots on your road?

What "unconscious competence" do you think you have that your harvest may bring to light? What will you discover when you begin unwrapping you?

CHAPTER 4:

On Defying Gravity

One of the women I spoke with told me a delightful story. When she was about 50, she attended a business meeting with several senior officers of the U.S. armed forces. She was the only woman there. At the end of the meeting, she remarked to one of the officers that it seemed uncomfortably warm in the room. The gentleman turned and looked at her. "Madam," he responded, "you are in menopause."

It had never occurred to this woman that she was in menopause, but when she thought about it, she realized that the general was right. Why did it take the power of the U.S. Army to bring this to her attention?

The woman was shocked, as much by the suggestion itself as by the forwardness of the man who made it. She said, rather indignantly, "Why would you say that, sir?"

He replied, "My wife is 60 and I recognize the symptoms of menopause when I see them. You removed and replaced your suit jacket five times in a 55-minute meeting! I repeat, madam, you are in menopause."

It had never occurred to this woman that she was experiencing the end of her reproductive cycle. But when she thought about it, she realized that the general was right—she was in menopause. Why did it take the power of the U.S. Army to bring this to her attention?

THE WORD IS MENOPAUSE, NOT MENOSTOP

I originally set out to study the changes that occur in a woman's life after the event of menopause. After speaking with just a few women I dropped the word *menopause* from the discussion because for Women of the Harvest, menopause appeared to be a nonevent. It simply came and went and was unremarkable, except for the loose change saved each month by not supporting the feminine-products industry.

The story I just told you took place 25 years ago. Now in her 70s, the woman who told it to me is still a dynamic force, working twelve hours a day in the pursuit of her chosen occupation. When I met her in person for the first time, there it was—the sparkle that signified a Woman of the Harvest.

Just for the record, in the time we were together she did not remove her jacket once.

For the Women of the Harvest, menopause is a nonevent—except for the loose change at the end of the month saved by not supporting the feminine-products industry.

It seems that passion for something greater than oneself is strong medicine that can be used to fight the woes of menopause. The women I spoke to who were in the midst of menopause could not understand what all the fuss was about. "An occasional inconvenience, nothing I can't deal with." Those who had passed it already said they had barely noticed its passing.

This cure works for other ailments too. When you have something in your life that fills you up and makes you feel good about yourself and your life, you have eliminated a lot of the barren space where worry and self-pity can fester and grow. Have you ever noticed how a common cold gets you more down now than it used to? Well, maybe the system is a little weaker and the symptoms take a greater toll. But remember when you were younger, "wifing," working, mothering, all three balls up in the air—a cold was simply something you did not have space in your life for.

You can choose to fill that space again with something that has meaning for you. One woman told me that learning dulls her aches and pains. Now bottle that one, Bayer! Current research exploring the relationship between mental activity and physical health in seniors supports the benefits of an active mind. Am I suggesting that you try Spanish lessons the next time your knees ache? Yes, that is exactly what I am suggesting. You may still have some pain, but think how great it will feel to be able to complain about your knees in another language.

> *One woman told me that learning dulls her aches and pains. Now bottle that one, Bayer!*

Of course, seeking professional advice to relieve some of the debilitating symptoms of age is appropriate, and there are advances in modern medicine that should not be ignored at this stage of a woman's life. If you can make your heart stronger, do so. If you can build your muscle so you can walk an extra mile, go for it. But don't confuse that sort of intervention—whether holistic or cutting-edge medical—with an obsession with removing all signs of aging.

What is the difference between fixating on breaking the laws of time and physics and working to have a fit and healthy body as you age?

One is an obsession, even an addiction, and it is bad for you. It doesn't take care of your life, it takes over your life. If you don't succeed in attaining your goal, you cease to be complete. The other is a good plan to enjoy life. It nurtures you and frees you to take on life as it comes, flexible, responsive, open, and aware.

If smoothing your facial lines lightens your perspective on life, go right ahead—free yourself in any way you can. If boosting that bone strength with medication brings you to the beach to play in the sand with your grandchildren, be present and enjoy. If a little estrogen in your coffee (or the prescribed equivalent) keeps your jacket on and your attention focused in the boardroom, sip and pop at will.

THE LIGHTNESS OF BEING 50+

The thighs do sag and, yes, the breasts are each day becoming more familiar with the territory of your tummy. But it's not just the outer body that the natural forces of gravity work on.

The body is the shell that houses you in life. Within this shell is a space—one person I interviewed described it as a well. This is a fitting image because we associate the well with knowledge, and this space is the container reserved for your knowledge of yourself.

Self-knowledge is a substance lighter than air,
and the more you have, the freer you are.
With enough you can fly!

When you are very young, this space inside you contains only self-knowledge. You act true to your nature, confident that this cannot be wrong, because it is who you are. What else can you do?

Very quickly, though, the error in your childish logic is pointed out and you are asked, if you are lucky—ordered, if you are not—to subscribe to the standards of conduct your society sets for you. You begin to fill the container once reserved for self-knowledge with the heavy material of rules, social structures, and instructions—norms designed as one size fits all and not unique to you. The trouble is that the size of the container is static, and as you grow and mature and your inner well fills up with the expectations of others, self-knowledge gets pushed into a smaller and smaller corner each day.

Self-knowledge is lighter than air, and the more you have, the freer you are. With enough you can fly!

But here is the good news. When aging starts to exert its gravitational pull, everything expands, not just the thighs and tummy. The well of self-knowledge gets deeper, and you can dig into the corners and unearth the pieces that got pushed aside over time. You can dig out what you knew to be true when you were five. You can dig out whatever made you sing before someone told you you were off key.

The light in the eyes of the Women of the Harvest is not just a visual effect. It is, to borrow a phrase from Milan Kundera, also experienced as "the incredible lightness of being". The deepening well of self-knowledge has become a limitless space. As the shell of the body softens, the weightless space inside increases, and with each revelation of self-knowledge and self-worth you get lighter. . . wow, what a diet!

THE LIGHT INSIDE

What kind of 50-year-old woman would Marilyn Monroe have been?

If Wikipedia had an entry for the light in a woman's eyes, the accompanying picture would definitely be Marilyn. But Marilyn did not make it to 50. What could she have learned along the way that would have helped her find her wisdom harvest?

(Okay, this is pure speculation. I never met the woman. But if you are going to write about the light in a woman's eyes, you have to include Marilyn.)

Men loved Marilyn's light—her smile, her sparkle—but my guess is that for Marilyn it was unconscious competence so it was not available to her as a resource in her private struggle for survival.

Perhaps not entirely unconscious—perhaps she knew that when she "sold" this light, things went well, she could get what she wanted, and other people were pleased, at least in the moment. But selling the light drained her because it was all an outflow. In the end she was quoted as saying that she was just too tired to keep going.

For the Women of the Harvest, even as their light engages those around them, it also turns back 180 degrees. It shines back inside, where it nurtures their confidence and sense of self; it re-energizes them until finally it consumes the body and the light is all there is. If you have had the privilege of sharing the last days and hours of a Woman of the Harvest you will have seen this phenomenon for yourself. You reach out to hold a hand, unsure if you will actually feel its weight in your own. It is the lightness of being free.

I speculate that what Marilyn never got a chance to understand was that her beauty was not her body—not the shell, but what the shell held.

What is it that draws the light back inside for some and not for others? What I heard in my interviews suggests that for some it takes courage—the courage to fail and to find something of yourself that is worthy in the humility of failure.

For others, it takes passion and the powerful drive to survive so that the passion may be realized. For a few, it seems to be a sense of mischief and humor about life that buoys them through the tough times and keeps everything in perspective. And let us not eliminate unexplainable luck, good fortune, grace.

I don't think Marilyn lived long enough to find any of those gifts within herself. It is a great loss. She would certainly have classed up the harvest festival.

DO I LOOK SEXY IN THIS BODY?

A while back we had a small dinner party. One of the guests was a 50-year-old man, now single, divorced for some time from his wife of 20 years and the mother of his three children. He is a kind man, and while I do not know him very well, I do like him. The conversation around the table turned to his love life. "So how is it going?" we asked. He responded with the news that he had a new interest. "Very beautiful, long blond hair and green eyes, like Kim Basinger—but not 50," he insisted. "Just 33."

I think it was the pride with which he said "33" that hit me the hardest. I gasped and spooned his dessert onto his plate with enough vigor to chip the bowl.

Someone once told me that it is the pretty ones who have the toughest time when their bodies start to change. Well, this was no time to find out I was pretty.

I could not understand what annoyed me—and I was annoyed and disappointed in this man. The more I thought about the incident, the more it spiraled into a big deep hole, a sort of questioning snake pit. What did he really mean?

And why do I care so much? And then, of course, the heavy personal questions . . . does this mean that at 50 pretty is gone and women my age are totally off the market for their male peers? And, and . . . help, get me out of this dark place!

Someone once told me that it is the pretty ones who have the toughest time when their bodies start to change. Well, this was no time to find out I was pretty. I never thought I was; it was not how I would have described myself. There was too much irony in discovering through this self-absorbed panic that I had been pretty, now that it seemed I no longer was nor could ever be again, at least in the perception of men . . . thank goodness, there must be a grain of sanity left if I could make that distinction.

If you paraded a group of men in front of me, ranging in age from 25 to 75, including Brad Pitt, Javier Bardem, Warren Beatty, and Sean Connery, and asked me which one was the best-looking, I can almost guarantee that I would pick Sean Connery or Warren Beatty, not one of the younger ones. I would pick Cary Grant in his later years, or Humphrey Bogart.

When I explained this to a friend of mine, he asked if these men were nude or clothed. "Clothed, of course," I responded, "When you think about women, do you only see them nude?" His answer was yes—and he believed that when most men saw a beautiful woman they imagined what she would look like naked.

So back to the question pit . . . if men examine women first as sex objects, then how is a woman past her physical prime ever to be seen for her beauty?

I sat with the questions. I thought about the Women of the Harvest and what they had told me. And I came to the realization that what was threatened in this situation was my sexuality. At the fine old age of 56, I was already fighting with the sense that it was changing. Much of my fantasy life was gone. (Well, I still fantasized about chocolate and ruling the world, but not so much about sex anymore.) While I enjoyed sex once it began, it was no longer a driving force in my life. On top of this change, I now had to face the fact that men, even men my age and older, would not find me as sexually attractive as a 33-year-old—and despite my own reduced interest in sex, men's reduced interest in me did not sit well.

Why does another person's response to me threaten my sexuality? Still in the pit, but the questions are getting better, don't you think?

In order to work out this latest question, I had to face some ugly realities about myself and how I used my sexuality in life. I share this for your sake, and if you think less of me when you finish, I consider the sacrifice worth it.

For years I had been showing up to play the game as I always had, bounding onto the field, ready to enjoy myself and the attention I would get. But lately something was very wrong. Somehow I was set apart from the rest, and I watched in a sort of sad reminiscent way as younger women got the attention I had hoped for. I was sidelined, more than sidelined: at least "sidelined" would have been a role with which to identify. I was in some sort of sexual no-man's-land (no pun intended). I could imagine myself turning to look over my shoulder and see if I was perhaps just standing behind myself, out of sight, because why else would people be looking right past me?

Surely there is nothing more insidiously selfish than a woman giving to fill her own need: blatant grasping dressed up as generosity.

One of the women I interviewed, when I asked what had changed in her life after 50, noted that she had given up skiing because she could no longer compete with the younger people. She was an athlete and her participation in sports was about winning. She had to be the best, so when she could no longer be, she sidelined herself. She left the ski hill and returned to horseback riding, which for her was not a competitive sport. Another woman told me, "There are no more prizes for just being there. So you don't have to compete if you really don't want to."

These comments made me worry even more.

As we age, are we supposed to give up sex like a sport on the theory that we're no longer at the top of our game? Well, I am not ready to give up sex. Damn it, I still feel sexy, somewhere—not sure where, it does seem to have moved, but *somewhere.*

Why does another person's response threaten my sexuality?

I tried to answer this question for myself as honestly as I could. What I discovered was that my sexuality up to this point had been externally driven. It was almost as if it did not belong to me at all; its quality and quantity were dependent on the reaction of others at every level, from simple conversation up to and including the sex act itself. Here's the really ugly truth: I had been treating my sexuality as a competitive weapon, using it to make myself feel better. But I was only competing with myself. Talking to a man, I can remember feeling my confidence boosted by the slightest flirtatious response. In bed, my partner's pleasure made me feel sexier and I became more responsive. I told myself this was my desire to please others—how unselfish of me. Surely there is nothing more insidiously selfish than a woman giving to fill her own need: blatant grasping dressed up as generosity.

In this process I had given my sexuality away, I had lost it for myself.

MORE THAN SKIN DEEP

I did not discuss sex with every woman I interviewed. I let the topic come up naturally rather than leading the women to it. (I thought that in itself could be interesting to observe.) But the Women of the Harvest, my mentors, answered all my questions—some in their words and some between the lines of their stories. They taught me that if you do not own your sexuality by the time its biological purpose is outlived, you will be left trying desperately to play in today's game using yesterday's equipment—which, by the way, seems to have changed only for you. Do you think you could score with a primitive club in a modern baseball game? You can swing that baby but you won't knock one out of the park.

If you don't own your sexuality by the time its
biological purpose is outlived, you will be left

trying to play in today's game using yesterday's equipment—which only seems to have changed for you.

We cannot help the fact that our sexuality, at some level, is part of every interaction we have. It is part of what we are. But when it becomes tied to our self-esteem it starts to show up in places that it really just should not be, and as we age things will get even more difficult.

Do not despair; remember the perfect design of aging? Like the light in a woman's eyes, as you age, your sex drive also turns 180 degrees and begins to pull you inward to a place where you are able to receive in a way you never dreamed you could. You become a taker, not a pseudo-giver, and in this honesty you find ecstasy again. What's more, in this honest vulnerability you are quite likely more capable than you ever have been of giving pleasure to your partner and engaging deeply with others without the static interference of sexual energy.

Desire arises, but it does not go "out there" to seek its validation; instead, somewhere deep inside you it stokes its own flame. The questions that arose before as your sexuality began to change now turn to knowing. It may be an unconscious knowing at the start, but in retrospect you will realize that you have answers from somewhere. You know you didn't ask anyone, not even yourself, "Am I sexy with this tummy, am I sexy with these thighs?" But your tummy, your thighs, and even your jiggly upper arms now scream out in joy, "Yes, I am sexy in this body"!

This beauty radiates from some knowing place inside a woman who has ceased to need the outer world to know herself.

If it seems that the sparkle in a Woman of the Harvest deepens with age, perhaps it's because her fire is fed in part by the internalization of sexual energy. This beauty is truly no longer skin deep. Instead, it radiates from some knowing place inside a woman who has ceased to need the outer world to know herself.

Note: A few weeks ago I had lunch with the gentleman I mentioned a few pages back. He is now enjoying a wonderful relationship with a woman 50+. His dessert was served this time with grace and no chipped china. I wish them both all the best in love and life.

REMBRANDT KNEW

In The Hermitage in Saint Petersburg, Russia, there is a Rembrandt painting titled Portrait of an Old Man in Red.

This painting is part of a series of Rembrandt's work he called "portrait biographies" and all the subjects of this period are older people. Rembrandt realized that within the lines and folds of the aged body the life of the person was contained. He would read the story the body offered and then transfer it onto canvas. In Portrait of an Old Man in Red the light focuses on the face and the hands. It is incredibly moving to look at what the artist has represented and emphasized by his use of light. The face and hands, which show so much of the wear and tear of living, have resisted darkness. They demand to be seen so the story of this life can be heard.

As I stood reading this visual biography, I asked myself why so many people choose to "iron out" their life stories. I imagine they think the fresh face is a great improvement, but I just see a blank canvas.

For Your Reflection

If you've gone through menopause or are going through it now, what impact has it made?

Do you notice that other people respond to you differently? What impact does that make on you?

Think about your own sexuality. How has it changed from one stage of your life to another? How is it changing now?

CHAPTER 5:

It's Called the Change of Life for a Reason

Change is the first hallmark of the years after 50. Various life routines begin to grind to a halt. Children are grown, careers have matured, and relationships are entering a new stage; couples turn and see each other differently as the "building" years wind down. There are no rules about what this change should look like. For some, this age marks the beginning of a period of travel, when long-deferred wanderlust can finally have free rein. For others, a lifetime of wanderlust ends and women feel for the first time a desire to come to roost in one location, maybe even returning to a place they have not called home for many years.

I asked the Women of the Harvest to talk about their experience of lifestyle changes after 50 and about the feelings that arose in them at that time in their lives. These are the stories they told.

Many women told me about people going out of their lives—divorce, widowhood, or the empty nest—but they also spoke about the new relationships that blossomed.

Careers were changed—particularly in the early 50s—because this phase was "finished," or there was "nothing left to learn" in that job, or they resented work that "sucked all the energy and gave nothing back," or they "just felt the need to do something new." They wanted to control their own time and they wanted different experiences outside their professional environments. Something had to give.

For many, after this transition period past 50, workplace success reached an all-time high. They spoke of being more respected than ever before, of doors tightly shut to them in their youth now opening. They spoke of their work as being more relevant than ever, with great meaning and sense of purpose; not coincidentally, they felt more financially stable, smarter and more emotionally resilient. Note: when I say past 50 I mean well past for some, 20 to 35 years.

Some women said they worked longer and harder than ever before; others said things had slowed, but there was a sense of relief, not loss, over this change in pace.

Many spoke about people going out of their lives—divorce, widowhood, or the empty nest—but they also spoke about the new relationships that blossomed. The common denominator in these new relationships was the need for a deeper connection with others. Friendship patterns changed as the need for more substantial connection changed the relationship landscape.

Some women said they worked longer and harder than ever before; others said things had slowed, but there was a sense of relief, not loss.

Homes changed too. Some realized the environments of their dreams, saying a cheerful goodbye to a place they had settled for and finally finding their perfect nest. One woman said with pride and courage and an overwhelming sense of acceptance, "I am living on my own for the first time in my life and I have no fear. I know the universe will look after me."

ALL THE WORLD'S A STAGE . . .
AND THESE ARE THE ROLES WE PLAY

I think Shakespeare had it right: this living we do is a play staged by the universe. We naturally slip into the roles life offers, and without so much as a read-through we boldly play out the scripts the grand agent presents.

The Women of the Harvest spoke of being daughters, sisters, mothers, wives, friends, employees, and bosses. The types of roles were not so different from one woman to the next and the roles did not change much with age. What was most interesting was the commonality of the women's relationships to their roles and how the relationships changed at the different stages of the actors' lives.

> *Before 50, there was a relentless drive to be the best. The world was full of right-way and wrong-way signposts.*

Roles played before 50 were played with intentionality. There was a strong sense of the work ethic required. Describing what it felt like to be in those roles, women used words like *responsibility* and *duty*. There was a strong drive to achieve in these roles, to succeed. Success meant becoming the best or the greatest mother, wife, manager, friend, or daughter-in-law. It did not matter if the script was for the workplace, the home, or the community. There was a relentless drive to be the best. There were standards and clear expectations for how things should be done. The world was full of right-way and wrong-way signposts and real and imagined report cards.

Not one woman I interviewed spoke of resenting the time spent in those roles, even though they all described in great detail the work, effort, and tension involved in keeping them all functioning efficiently. One woman described herself as "a well-trained, loyal dog," unquestioning in her obedience to the requirements of the roles she played.

The roles, it seemed, were what society expected of women, and the women playing them perceived them as essential to someone else: "The children needed my attention," "My husband was dependent on me," "My boss was incapable of figuring this out for herself." At the same time, they spoke of their own neediness, of how playing these roles was essential to their sense of self-worth.

They also spoke about their hesitancy to seek help from others to fulfill their roles. What is this about women? They would gladly help a peer if she asked—which she wouldn't, because women don't ask for help with the things they "should" know how to do. Why do we believe we should somehow magically just know how to . . . go ahead, fill in the blank?

> *Why do women believe we should*
> *somehow magically know how to . . .*
> *go ahead, fill in the blank?*

Where is it written, for example, that the act of childbirth makes you a skilled parent? At least in the workplace we proactively offer skill development. A new manager will be trained in how to delegate. Who trains the new mother to delegate or communicate her needs to her life partner? "Dear, I need you to get the groceries on Saturday while I do the laundry and make a week's supply of puréed peas."

THE SEED OF SELF

The Women of the Harvest claimed to be fully identified with these roles they played before their 50th birthdays. But I came away from the interviews with the strong sense that if I had done them 20 or 30 years ago and probed into what made these women tick, they would most likely not have defined themselves just by these roles they played. They would have described some small, fleeting sense of something else, some other aspect of identity.

So how did things change after 50?

One woman's insightful observation gives us a clue: "At some point I noticed that while I felt fully involved in the many and varied roles I played in my youth, there was some part of me that remained constant, that had not changed as I jumped from one role to the other."

One day she looked up and noticed that the landscape had shifted. Suddenly there was space in her life.

Here is a look behind the curtain to a woman's sense of self, growing stronger every day and quietly supporting her in the role-playing life required. Each day and each year she perceived more "me" and less role.

Simultaneously, the roles themselves changed over time. Then one day she looked up and noticed that the landscape had shifted. Suddenly—though of course it was the kind of "suddenly" that took 30 years to manifest— there was space in her life.

This is a critical milestone on the path to the harvest celebration. It is here, at this time in a woman's life, that we can first study what differentiates those who embrace the 50+ years and those who don't. The "me" that stays constant in all the roles of life is the seed of self, present within you from birth till death. It is the life force that animates you. As you lose yourself in the roles you must play, it does not change or fade or leave, but rests quietly inside you.

> *The "me" that stays constant in all the roles of life is the seed of self, present within you from birth till death.*

When you read that expression, lose yourself, you may nod and think you understand what I am saying. But what does lose your self really mean? Of course the self cannot truly be lost as in "disappeared", but it can be lost as in *damn, where did I leave that thing?* And the degree to which the self gets "lost" varies. Some women don't ever really lose track of this self identity; it is always there in the background and each life experience feeds it. Others lose touch with it completely while they "become" their roles. Why one experience for some and a different one for others? I cannot explain the workings of the universe. I know only what I have observed: there are two different kinds of women who reach the 50-year milestone.

There are those who believe that they are what they do. They think of themselves as having become the roles they have played—daughter, mother, accountant. For these women, the space revealed when life's roles shift is empty and threatening. They look out on an ever-extending personal timeline and apply what Barbara Morris calls the "flat earth view of life." In other words, what we cannot see over the horizon is unknown and therefore cannot possibly be something to which we should look forward. Christopher Columbus, who took a different view, did not fall off the edge of the earth into nothingness when he sailed as far as anyone in Spain could see . . . instead he got a marvelous surprise!

The Women of the Harvest don't fear the horizon and don't notice a void in their lives at all. Their matured sense of self effortlessly fills up the space created when their roles change. They know what and who they are, both apart from and within the roles they play. When they look out at the same personal timeline extending past their well-planned and tightly scheduled years, they embrace the opportunity it offers. Remember, these are the women who did not notice menopause—it was a non-issue for them, simply an inconvenience removed. Now, as their roles change. perhaps fall away, there may be loss, but there is no emptiness.

THE "ME" INSIDE THE ROLE

Of course, many of the roles in a woman's life continue after 50. The majority of women I interviewed still play the same roles they played in their 20s, 30s, and 40s; they are still parents to their children, still partners to their partners, still as engaged as ever in their work. What's remarkable about the Women of the Harvest is their *relationship* to these roles at this stage.

While pre-50 role-playing was intentional, now it is spontaneous. The actions required flow naturally, without tension. Women describe themselves as comfortable in their roles, comfortable with the unknown and unplanned aspects of life and the opportunities they may bring, unburdened by codes of right and wrong or that incessant need to please someone else. They say they are free, doing things because they want to, not because they have to or they are expected to. One woman described this time to me as "a new-found freedom" in which she felt able to "explore myself outside the roles which had previously defined me."

Enormous courage comes from this freedom and the willingness to experience.

The Women of the Harvest accept all the times and stages of their lives for what they are at the point of delivery.

The Women of the Harvest seem to have used this courage to break free not only from the judgments of others but from the need to judge and measure themselves. They make absolutely no critical comparisons between their lives and roles before and after 50. No one I interviewed said, "I loved that time best" or "I am a better person now." They accept all the times and stages of their lives for what they are at the point of delivery. This non-judgmental view of life is one of the strongest distinguishing features of the Women of the Harvest. These women loved the all-consuming drive to achieve world-class status (as mother or lawyer or both) in their younger years as much as they love the freedom and spontaneity they find in their 70s.

As Madeleine L'Engle so wisely put it, "The great thing about getting older is that you don't lose all the other ages you've been."

But though they don't compare their roles then and now, they do experience them differently. They do not see themselves as essential in the roles they play, but this is not a loss of status, because the role itself is not essential to their sense of worth. In other words, they are valuable in and of themselves, with or without the roles, and now the sense of self does not need to be fed by the role.

I think the roles are performed differently, too. As we become less concerned about what others think of us, we are more able to let go of our need to control because we do not claim the success of others as our own accomplishment. Our faith in others to perform and make choices increases, as does our faith in our own natural abilities and skills. Tension and worry diminish and our ability to delegate and to educate increases. The Women of the Harvest use the words *advisors* and *counselors* to describe themselves when before they called themselves *managers* and *directors*.

My sister has recently become a grandparent. She is one of the best mothers I know, but this grandparent thing seems to be a quantum leap in joy. Could it be the free, spontaneous, uncritical approach to the role that makes it so rich and full?

As Madeleine L'Engle put it, "The great thing about getting older is that you don't lose all the other ages you've been."

One Woman of the Harvest put it this way: before 50, she was "being the roles," and after 50, she was "putting on the clothes of the roles."

Another told me that post-50 the life roles she played "seemed less black and white, more gray, gray like twilight."

THE TIGHTROPE OF FEMININITY

The Women of the Harvest tell me that the roles they play 50+ enact a greater sense of balance. Hallelujah!

In my corporate coaching practice, so many of my female clients ask for help with that very issue. "Help me to balance my work life and my home life . . . my life as a wife and as a mother . . . when do I get time for my friends?"

I am actually beginning to believe that most of their lives are balanced—balanced by the very sense of self, always present, that centers their lives. In our early lives this self may be so little known to us, so imperceptible, that as we jump from role to role we perceive ourselves as completely

GRAYLIGHT

There is a certain kind of light that comes late, at the end of the day, when colors are traded in for sepia tones. It has long been my favorite time. It is best experienced over water, this graying of the daylight, this twilight hour.

For the first second or so it seems that everything within your sight has peacefully settled into one. The distinguishing vibrancy of the day is gone, but you are captivated.

Twilight does not hold the warming promise of sunrise or the exciting full-on light of noon. It is subtle, and we can easily overlook it as just the ending of light, the beginning of darkness. But when we experience it this way, we lose it as a time of its own. It becomes lost time. Do you have time to lose?

You need to stop to see the graying time. It takes some study to discover and appreciate all the shades it contains.

If you want the sunny day to last longer, you will resent the graying, and if you are afraid of the approaching dark you will want to quickly turn on the lights.

If, however, you can sit still in this muted time, you can share its peace. You may discover not a transition period from one thing you know to another you fear, but a beauty unto itself.

at the mercy of the needs of others, forces outside ourselves. We think this means we can't possibly be balanced, as if balance is something only we can create for ourselves.

The women I interviewed, because of their age range, together have the ability to see the bigger picture of how balance works over a lifetime. After listening to what they had to tell me I propose the following; what if balance is not something you need to create? What if the way you commit to those roles and play them with all your heart and energy at 20, 30, and 40 is precisely the balanced way of the world? What if, while you play these roles, deep inside you without your knowledge or attention your sense of self is getting stronger and creating more stability for you every day?

Have faith—you've got your balance already.

Balance comes from stability. The more stable, and centered something is, the more balanced it will be. A well-designed automobile or a self-aware working woman can hug the unexpected curves that the road throws, turn on a dime, and gracefully roll right over those speed bumps if need be. Think about it, for the most part you're doing exactly that . . . hugging, turning and rolling right along . . .

have faith, you've got your balance. You will come to know it in your years after 50. Now isn't that a reason to look forward to your birthday?

GIRLFRIEND!

Let's take a moment to recap. Women are very skilled at giving themselves to the functions they perform, the roles they have taken on, the partners they love, the children they nurture, and the jobs they are passionate about. Then, at 50, some time and a little space suddenly open up—they look up and discover that something's missing. As my wise mentor once said to me, "Girlfriend, you need girlfriends!"

Maybe it sounds a little redundant, but you get the point and so did I. We do need girlfriends; we are herd creatures. Some of us like big herds and others prefer what would be better described as a pair than a herd, but there is something about friendship that is not reproducible with spouses or children or even siblings, no matter how good those other relationships may be.

When I began interviewing women about life 50+, I didn't include a question about friendships. I had no idea they would change during a woman's life. I always thought some people were good at making friends and keeping them and some people were not. I considered friendship "styles" an attribute of personality, not a function of age.

As the pressure of adult roles eases, women feel a natural urge to be known again as Sue, May, or Karen, not as CFO, Mrs. Smith, or even Mom.

The Women of the Harvest had something to teach me here. It was almost unanimous among the women I spoke to: friendships change after 50. Women no longer feel obligated to spend time with people because it is a social responsibility, the right thing to do. They lose their tolerance for superficial connection; they may seek new friends with whom they can connect more significantly while they let long-standing but less substantial friendships ebb. Many reunite with old friends, from college or even childhood.

Why these "retro relationships"? I imagine that as the pressure of adult roles eases, women feel a natural urge to spend time with people who knew them before they were consumed by those roles. They can be known again as Sue, May, or Karen, not as CFO, Mrs. Smith, or even Mom—they can be reminded of the *self* contained, perhaps buried, deep in the role-play.

These changes are an important part of the preparation for the harvest. The harvest is important work, and the harvesters are women. They know that to do a job right, you not only have to show up, work hard, and use the right tools, you also need the right outfit and the right accessories.

The Women of the Harvest find new friendships the way a woman with a well-stocked closet selects a new purse. She knows exactly what she wants, but there is no urgency. If and when the right thing shows up, she will give it a place of honor and treasure it for a long time because it was so well and carefully chosen.

Just in case you may think I have reduced friends to accessories, let me explain. Women are almost anatomically attached to their purses. We may trade in a big leather tote for a belly pack or a wallet-size clutch or even just a pocket in a suit, but the purpose that space serves in our life never goes away. Just like our friends, it is essential and we hesitate to go far without it.

Now, just as we have earned the good taste to know cheap shoes from Italian–designed and great wine from boxed, we have higher standards for friendship as well.

While we were striving in our youth to be the best at everything, we didn't have to be so selective in our friendships. Now, just as we have earned the good taste to know cheap shoes from Italian-designed and great wine from boxed, we have higher standards for friendship as well. The Women of the Harvest choose wisely, disentangling themselves from things that may hold them back from the task at hand and people for whom this time of life is barren, not bountiful.

How many women 50+ do you know who are cleaning out closets, selling big houses, and lugging a lifetime of collectibles onto the driveway for a garage sale?

It seems the intuitive pull to lighten the load for the time ahead is very strong. When the bag is repacked, it is amazingly light. In these new, deeper connections and in the revitalized friendships of youth, the Women of the Harvest find once again that more can become magically less—less weight, less struggle, less drag. Their lives continue, roles reshaping as they go along but enhanced and refreshed by the new relationships . . . just like a great new bag can totally revitalize an old outfit!

For Your Reflection

Think about the roles you have played at different points in your life. Were you acting for other people's benefit? Who was depending on you, and how did it make you feel?

How much do your roles define you? Would you say you are "being" the roles or "putting on the clothes"?

Think about the seed of self, the "me" inside all your roles. How have you kept this in view over the years? How do you see it now?

CHAPTER 6:
To Begin Again & Again

U p to this point I have focused on introducing you to the Women of the Harvest, bringing you the voices of women who embrace aging. I did this to offer you an alternative outlook on getting older, in the hope that in the stories and wisdom of these women you would find inspiration to begin your own harvest.

I believe that this stage of life is a natural stage of female human development. I think every woman has within herself the potential to be a Woman of the Harvest. Given our basic natures and our life circumstances, we will develop our harvest attitude to varying degrees—but even a single basket full of harvest wisdom can enrich our lives.

So how do you get there?

START WHERE YOU ARE

In my role as a corporate leadership consultant, I am hired to either, worst-case scenario, "fix" someone's leadership skills or, best-case, enhance them. Basically, I am in the business of facilitating the development of attitudes and skills that can enhance people's lives. I work with what I call the revelation theory of education. The root of the word *educate* is the Latin word *educere*, meaning "to draw out." Education does not mean to fill; it never meant that, though we often talk about it as if it did. We are not empty vessels to be filled by educators armed with information. Instead, we contain within ourselves the answers and the knowledge we need. The role of the educator is to skillfully draw out that knowledge—or enable us to draw it out ourselves—so we can use it in our lives.

How well do you know yourself? Have you really checked that out recently? Some things do change, and there may be some aspects of your nature that are still unknown to you. The revelation theory works particularly well when we are talking about using self-knowledge for development. And my theories on development are a bit different than the current popular philosophy that we can create the life we want. I believe that the life we get, which is changing every moment, is the product of the nature we were born with

135

and that nature's response to the spontaneous events that come into our lives.

How well do you know yourself?
Have you really checked that out recently?

It may seem that we bring about many of those events ourselves, but when we look more deeply, we see that our actions and reactions are informed by our nature, which was imprinted at birth. We woke up in this world already loaded with most components of our operating system, and while it evolves as we take the imprint of our conditioning, we are still acting and reacting very much out of that basic nature. This nature, by the way, is not good or bad, just unique. So even if you react to an unplanned event in what you think is a conscious way, you are still reacting through your operating system; you have no other choice. Therefore, your reaction is really rooted in your basic nature, in what is natural to you. There is great value in under-standing what is natural in our lives, the characteristics of our personal operating system.

To sum all that up . . . work with what you have. There is great material there!

CHANGE YOUR PERSPECTIVE

You are already well on your way to becoming a Woman of the Harvest if you have gotten this far in this book. You have been immersed in these women's alternative perspective on aging, and you have probably been checking off the characteristics you already possess and noting those you still desire. In the pages ahead I hope to help you get even closer to your harvest wisdom.

If we don't have a positive outlook on the destination, where do we get the energy to keep going? How can you act your age if you are afraid of it?

First, I'd like you to think about your attitude toward aging and what is influencing that attitude. The attitude of the Women of the Harvest requires a fundamental change in the way we perceive and therefore value aging. Changing our view of life is not easy, but I have faith that we will support each other to do this. If we don't have a positive outlook on the destination, where do we get the energy to keep going? How can you act your age and so reap its benefits if you are afraid of it? In modern culture, the prevalent attitude about getting older is not, for the

137

most part, positive. Some of the reasons for this negative attitude may no longer be justified, but it's understandable that they persist. Let's examine a few.

We have few positive role models for aging. But look around—more and more are appearing every day in the mainstream media. There are now many publications geared to the 50+ market that extol the virtues of life over 50 and what can be accomplished within it. The media is changing the focus from age per se to lifestyle, and the concept of lifestyle does not carry the same negative associations as aging. Check out *Zoomer*, a Canadian publication intended to replace the more sedate Canadian Association for Retired Persons monthly. Glossy and fun, billing itself as "Canada's Lifestyle Magazine for Boomers," *Zoomer* is a big step in the right direction. In the U.S., More magazine is devoted to women 40+; a recent issue carried the tagline "Celebrating What's Next." In the U.K., *Woman & Home* purposefully addresses women at "all ages and stages," and it shows in everything from the advertising to the cover photos.

We dislike aging in part for one very simple reason: we love living. Since we know that aging will eventually lead to the end of living, it's no wonder we try our very hardest to slow it down.

We also equate the changes of aging with decline and loss. Well, yes, life ends, and change brings small "ends" along the way, but we can't stop that inevitability by deciding not to participate in life. Think how much we would miss. Picture yourself eating an amazing piece of chocolate torte with fresh raspberry sauce dripping over the dark chocolate ganache. Each delicious mouthful, its own little "foodgasm," also takes you closer to the last bite. Wouldn't it be a shame if your worry over the eventual disappearance of that treat kept you from enjoying every yummy morsel? "Yes, but," you say to yourself, "the cake is good. Aging is not." But wait—we've agreed that you enjoy life now. That's why you don't want it to end. Why have you convinced yourself you will not enjoy the 50+ years just as much as you have enjoyed all the previous ones? The 20s, 30s, and 40s also had their ups and downs . . . remember?

Here's the real irony. All the effort that goes into fear of aging and strategies to delay it is energy misspent—but still spent. It will exhaust you, and you will end up without the resources you need to deal with things that changed in spite of you while you were busy resisting.

We look at folks who are older than we are, see the general physical decline, pick up a few moans and grumbles from them as they go by, and think, "Great, that's really something to look forward to." We imagine their internal state, their attitude and their satisfaction with life, based on how they appear externally. Then we make the leap to how we assume we will feel internally when we reach that physical state. The Women of the Harvest are telling us that when we look at it that way we are missing something important—something that significantly impacts the quality of life for older women, something that goes much deeper than physical concerns. Our heroines have a perspective on getting old that is not the common one but serves them very well. I think more of us should join them.

I WONDER WHAT HE EXPECTED

*On my parents' 70th wedding anniversary, a reporter from
the local paper came to the house to interview them. My parents,
91 and 94 at the time, lived on their own. My dad still drove,
they cooked for themselves, and they had only occasional help
with the housecleaning. They read everything the local library
could supply in large print and they both painted with oils. My
father worked in a woodshop creating gaggles of wonderful
hand-carved birds that still sit on our hearths. My mother
knitted and played the piano. Dad digested the daily paper
and two weekly national news magazines and could argue
every point from every article. My mother could still beat her
grandchildren at billiards or gin rummy.*

*After the reporter had completed the interview, he left looking
stunned. He muttered something to me at the door about how
great my parents were, then went off to wrestle with his own
challenged perspective on aging.*

*The moment the door closed, my mother turned to me
in complete disgust. "He expected us to be propped up
and drooling!"*

All the effort that goes into fear of aging and strategies to delay it is energy misspent—but still spent. It will exhaust you, and you will end up without the resources you need.

How much have you really bought into this negative perspective? Is your perspective on aging outdated and not very flattering anymore? You wouldn't wear last season's fashions unless you believed they still suited you, would you? Do your views on getting older suit you? Do they suit the woman you have become, and will they serve the way you want to live for the next 40, 50, or 60 years? That's a long time to be wearing out-of-date slacks.

We perceive the world through our senses, but our mind processes what we see with the knowledge collected there. This explains why you may literally be unable to see or hear something that is right in front of you: your mind does not contain the information that would enable it to process the experience, or it contains information that distorts what you are seeing with some preconceived notion about how things should be in that moment. If our mind holds a negative image of aging, then when we begin to recognize the signs of aging in ourselves, we seek to be young again and to bring back the old days. Turning back the clock seems the only solution for our dissatisfaction with our changing reality. We don't see going forward as a solution, because our negative perceptions of aging are clouding our thinking. The preoccupation with gaining back what we had turns us away from our future. Staring longingly at our past, we cannot see the gifts that a new perspective on life could offer.

Do your views on getting older suit you? Will they serve the way you want to live for the next 40, 50, or 60 years? That's a long time to be wearing out-of-date slacks.

When our fundamental perspective on aging shifts, a whole new world opens up. Now we can embrace our age, whatever it is, and its inherent rewards. The Women of the Harvest are free to receive the daily events of life 50+ as they come, some bad, some good, but not pre-interpreted in a way that skews their experience of the balance between the two.

GET COMFORTABLE WITH CHANGE

Next, you need to think about how you react to change, because 50+ is going to involve change—change you cannot stop. We can slow aging, briefly cheat it, and of course try to ignore it, but the only way to stop it is to die.

Joan Erikson, whom we met in chapter 2, tells us that we must be willing to begin again and again over the course of a lifetime, and when you think about it that is exactly what we do. We have lots of practice beginning again and again. We have been married, divorced, and remarried, we have birthed and raised and then empty-nested, we have been hired, fired, and rehired, born in one country, raised in another, and living in a third. We have sometimes failed and sometimes succeeded but always kept going. We have endured loss that has changed the landscape of our lives and hearts forever, and still we have kept going.

> *Over the course of a lifetime,*
> *we must be willing to*
> *begin again and again.*

Erikson, the author of several books on life and living, is the poster-child for the Women of the Harvest.

Well into her 90s she was exploring, learning, and building. Shortly before her death at the age of 95, she published again. She had written an extended version of *The Life Cycle Completed*, a book describing the stages of human development that she and her husband, Erik Erikson, had collaborated on many years before. She suggested that she was driven to complete the new version of the book because, having reached the final stage of her own life, she realized there was more to say. I believe her need to keep using the wisdom she had harvested in her life stayed strong until her very last days.

If we had the wisdom to realize that each breath is a beginning, and that, whether the last moment was a win or a loss, the next moment is all new, then we would have nothing to fear in Joan Erikson's wise counsel on beginning again and again. Because while the landscape may be constantly changing, each moment offers us a chance to do our best again, and we are "armed" in each new moment with the accumulated experience and wisdom of all the moments that came before it.

In this journey we call life there are plateaus, like rest stops that are comfortable, satisfying, and safe—and sometimes the view from there is even magnificent—but then the journey must continue. You can enjoy the shade and the view for a while, but you cannot take up permanent residence in one of those smooth roadside spots. If you are breathing, you are changing, and so is everything around you.

The fact that everything around you is changing is actually the good news. There is no big heroic decision to make here—"I will sign up for the change team!" You are going to change as you live. Change is not variable. The variable is you—your acceptance or resistance of that change.

If we had the wisdom to realize that each breath is a beginning, and that, whether the last moment was a win or a loss, the next moment is all new, then we would have nothing to fear.

Ask yourself, "What is it I am resisting today?" Make that "What am I resisting today *besides my age*"—I suggest you start with something a little bit smaller than your own mortality to begin building your tolerance. Is it something in the world of technology? Is it your parents getting older? Is it a move to a new neighborhood?

Or is the change you resist more subtle, more like a change in thinking?

Do you resist understanding:

Your grandson's taste in clothes?

Your co-worker's political views?

Your husband's new fascination with motorcycles?

Are you clinging to some belief about a right way or a wrong way that you have not actually checked out for validity in years?

It's trying to stand still that makes the rest of the world look as if it is flying by at breakneck speed. What would happen if you could let change flow around you and through you at the same pace as it always has? If you weren't firmly rooted to your fear that change equals loss, you could bob and roll with it all much easier. The speed limit hasn't changed, ladies; it just looks that way when you are stopped on the shoulder. Merge back in, slowly at first, and see where it gets you. The view may be even better from there.

The speed limit hasn't changed, ladies;
it just looks that way when you are stopped on the
shoulder. What would happen if you could let change
flow around you and through you at the same pace as
it always has?

JUMPERS, SITTERS, AND DIGGERS— WHICH ONE ARE YOU?

Our reaction to change is linked to our personality type. If I take some poetic license, I can divide people into three types according to the way they face change:

- Heel Diggers
- Fence Sitters
- Early Jumpers

Heel Diggers cling to what they believe is the present but in reality has already become the past. At the extreme, they might admit to preferring death to change. They have shut down their logic receptors, so it is difficult to give them the information they need to consider the advantages of change.

It may seem to them that it's easier to lie down and let progress march over their graves than to learn to use an iPhone, consider driving a Smart Car, or accept footless tights as suitable attire for a dinner party.

To a Heel Digger, it seems easier to lie down and let progress march over her grave than to learn to use an iPhone.

Fence Sitters—I never understood these folks—it can't be comfortable. But perhaps some may have sat up there balancing on the pickets for so long that they imagine they are in a comfy armchair. Or maybe they're just numb.

From the fence, in theory, they can see both sides, where they came from and where they could go. You would think that with such a panoramic view it would be easier to chose a side, and some Fence Sitters do eventually, but others are truly stuck . . . impaled in their position. Again I wonder, how comfortable can that be? Obviously it's more comfortable than making a decision.

Early Jumpers, on the other hand, grab on quickly to new theories and are the first to move into the new world. The risks of danger in the new order don't seem to bother them. Sometimes they even jump a little too soon—but they are flexible and can usually jump back or jump somewhere else. Early jumpers like change, so it is easier for them, and if change is not happening quickly enough to suit them, they sometimes initiate it.

Many of the Women of the Harvest are Early Jumpers, but some, by their natures, fall into the category of Fence Sitters. The difference was they jumped off those fences and moved on just before things got too painful. I did not find any

Women of the Harvest who were Heel Diggers, because by definition they do not move on—or if they do, they're the very last to—and this is not the way of our harvest women.

Sure, the women I interviewed struggled and grumbled with new technologies, fashions, and politics as much as anyone, but in the end these were not barriers, just hurdles. The Women of the Harvest pick themselves up, work around or over or under the problem, reinvent, redesign, and keep going.

The women I interviewed struggled and grumbled with new technologies, fashions, and politics as much as anyone, but in the end these were not barriers, just hurdles.

CONSIDER YOUR CHOICES

Aging is not a choice. It comes uninvited, and as with many of our body's tricks and turns, we cannot opt out. No matter what control freaks we may admit to being and no matter how effective we think we have been in that role, we cannot stop this natural process. However, within this time of change there are choices to make.

When we were in our 20s and 30s, we built our lives step by step, making decisions about how to earn a living, where to do that living, with whom to share that living, and the shape and style of that life. Then, for the most part, we got on with it. There were course corrections along the way. Things changed—sometimes mildly, sometimes drastically —and we had adjustments to make. But for the most part we were so busy living the life that we perceived less choice. How many times have you said, "I'm too busy to think about that"? That is the "getting on with it" I am describing.

When the big 5-0 knocks on the door, we start to realize that this may mark a new era in our lives. We see that for the first time in many years there will be major decisions to make, and soon—decisions about issues we have had on automatic pilot for many years.

The choices we will have to make at this age are basically the same ones we made earlier. If we begin to look at them in our early 50s, we will have lots of time to nail down decisions. But if you blew out your 50 candles many years ago, there is no need to panic. It is never too late to make conscious choices to live the best life available to you . . . so start today, whatever age you are.

At 50, we see that there will be major decisions to make, and soon—decisions about issues we have had on automatic pilot for many years.

A word of caution is required here. We make decisions because that is how we function in the world, but we must never forget about chance. Chance will change our decisions and turn their consequences upside down. Sometimes it makes life more difficult than we ever expected; sometimes it brings wonderfully unexpected gifts our way too. So go ahead and make your choices, just leave a little space in your calendar for chance . . . now, pass the dice, please.

These are the choices you will make in your 50s and 60s:

- When do I want to retire and what do I want to do when I am retired? Is it retire or retread? Is it golf or can I really have that dog breeding business I always wanted? Is it time to go back to school for fun? Do I need to work part-time?

- Keep the house or sell it? Trade the big condo for a smaller place? Stay in the city or move to the lake?

Move from the country to the city? Will I want these stairs or this garden when I am 80? How much travel do I want to do or can I afford to do, and how does that affect where I should live?

Where are the grandchildren, and do I want to be closer? What do I need to do to assist my aging parents? Could I live so far from our friends, and where will I make new ones?

Even our intimate relationships can come up for decision-making at this time. Sometimes, sadly, in the thinking space that opens up past 50 we see that a long-lived marriage is less than we had hoped. Or we may find our partnership to be very rich and full—we've just been taking it for granted a little bit too much and we need to take a fresh approach. *This* kind of change can be a lot of fun.

Nature has generously given women this significant physiological event, menopause, to mark the gateway into the rest of our lives. Yes, those hot flashes are really warning lights. Perhaps the word *menopause* was originally created to suggest a time to *pause* for a moment—to think, evaluate, and assess. Without menopause we might slip into the 50+ years without realizing we are on the threshold of a new era and we have some preparation to do—without taking this time to harvest the knowledge that will nourish the rest of our lives.

In the thinking space that opens up past 50, we may see that a long–lived marriage is less than we had hoped. Or we may find that our partnership is very rich and full—we just need to stop taking it for granted.

For the Women of the Harvest, as I mentioned earlier, the event of menopause really wasn't all that significant, and without my pestering questions I believe many would have remained unconscious of their knowledge harvest too. They just soldier on in life, almost magically integrating their self-knowledge and wisdom and with no apparent effort transforming their attitude toward life. Some of us are more battered by the physical change of menopause, but the good news is this gives us an opportunity to make a more conscious effort to move through the gateway and start reaping our rewards. However, even the Women of the

Harvest make changes in their lives at this stage, and I believe that those changes—in career and relationships and living space, in many things—are informed by their unconscious wisdom. They lose little or no energy to the concerns of aging; change is noted, lived, accepted, and they move on.

Chances are you are going to have to work a bit harder to harvest your knowledge and integrate it into your life. In the next chapter we'll think more about knowledge, how we relate to it, and the role it plays in our lives.

For Your Reflection

What is your basic perspective on aging? What do you think informs it?

How do you respond to change—are you a Heel Digger, a Fence Sitter, or an Early Jumper? Do you embrace certain kinds of change and resist others?

What choices are you facing, or have you faced, as you approach or pass 50?

CHAPTER 7:

Your Knowledge Harvest

Knowledge comforts me. Knowledge tells me I have lived, like knowing it is autumn just by the sound of crisp leaves underfoot or that certain smell in the air. I can name those smells and sounds because I have lived them; they are part of my living experience, they are familiar.

Knowledge is the harvest of my experience and it suggests there is order in life even when I cannot understand that order. When we understand that knowledge comes from life experience, then we see that what was difficult to live through in the past was worthwhile and even what was easy had value.

Knowledge tells me I have lived, like knowing it is autumn just by the sound of crisp leaves underfoot or that certain smell in the air.

Much of our knowledge is tacit, and that is often a blessing. How could we drive, talk on the phone (hands-free, of course), drink coffee, and follow the ever-patient voice of our GPS if the knowledge that directed our driving was not tacit? But when we pull that tacit knowledge up to the surface, we are able to apply it in a whole new way, doubling or even tripling its value. For example, in order to teach someone else to drive, you needed to bring your tacit knowledge about driving out into the open, review it, and reframe it in such a way that it could be shared.

So it is with the knowledge harvest that begins at 50. It will take some work, some digging and pulling, because much of what you have accumulated may not be at the surface of your conscious mind. It is, after all, harvest time, traditionally a time of hard and sustained work. Fortunately, we have the gift of menopausal zest, that burst of hormonal energy to boost us. So take a deep breath and start digging.

YOUR TRUE STORY

This is your harvest; indeed, you *are* the harvest as you come to know yourself. There will be magic to help you unearth it—not black or white magic, but transparent magic. The magic only happens when you begin to see clearly through your own beliefs, desires, and actions.

This is your harvest; indeed, you are the harvest
as you come to know yourself.

As much as you can, observe yourself with detachment and curiosity. The work of this observation may quiet that pesky judgmental commentary rattling through your brain, rounding your shoulders, and dropping your chin. Consider this harvest exercise emotional aerobics. Lift your head, ladies, and observe: look to the right and to the left and see who you are today. Stretch back, opening your chest and your heart, then fold forward, wrapping your arms around yourself in a hug.

In the silence of observation and the space your self-awareness creates, your true story starts to unfold before your eyes. You discover your nature and you begin to see your actions and thoughts and feelings for what they are. And you start living those phrases we all know: "Oh, that's just the way she is," "that's the way it is," "live with it."

We so often hear those sayings as cop-outs. In fact, they are some of the wisest words spoken. When you really know that this is just the way you are, just the way he or she is, just the way things are, acceptance has taken root— and acceptance and judgment cannot grow in the same soil.

I saw that wisdom at work in the life of one woman who told me her story. She was nervous as she spoke, like a young teenager in her first high heels, a little unsure on her feet, and each stolen glance my way had a small questioning look to it.

The story went like this. She had struggled at work; it was stressful, a bad boss, increasing demands. She cared, but the cost was too high. She was surviving in the job moment to moment, counting each second there like it was a week of her life. The sleepless nights began. Soon she found herself lying awake at 2 a.m. on a Sunday morning worrying about work.

So she sought help. I did not get the details on that. All I heard were the results.

Along the path to recovery, she learned about herself. She learned how she functioned, what traits were natural to her, and what traits she had adopted in reaction to her life so far.

The day I met this lady, she had begun to shine. A small glimmer of light was spreading on her tentative face. She looked me in the eye and said, "All I know is: today I am 54

STYLE FOR THE JOURNEY

*If this whole farming metaphor is just too earthy for you, here's
an alternative. Think of your knowledge harvest as the discovery
of a new perspective on your personal style—not just fashion
but your whole lifestyle. Your style includes: how you dress,
the textures and colors in your wardrobe, how you shape and
decorate the environment in which you live, how and where you
choose to spend your time and even with whom you spend it,
what you read, what movies you see, what charities and causes
you support, how you define beauty—all the aspects that others
use to recognize you and even to know you. Style develops day
to day and year to year as you make decisions in accordance*

with your nature and in response to what life brings. Then one day you wake up and voilà! You have a unique personal style.

Do you know what your personal style is? Could you describe it to someone who had never seen you? Like tacit knowledge made explicit, personal style discovered makes packing for the rest of the journey much more effective. So if you prefer, think of your 50s and 60s as the preparation stage for a trip that will begin in earnest a bit later on. We don't want to get caught at 70, 80, or 90 with a suitcase full of outfits we hate because we didn't give enough thought to the packing, now do we?

years old and I want to live to be 108 because I have never felt better in my whole life than I do today."

She was still in the same job. Nothing had changed—or had it?

When you really know that this is just the way you are, just the way he or she is, just the way things are, acceptance has taken root—and acceptance and judgment cannot grow in the same soil.

YOUR PERSONAL INVENTORY

So far in this book you have checked out your attitude toward aging, described your relationship to change, and come to understand the value of self-awareness—just for starters. All this exploration has been encouraged by the voices of the Women of the Harvest and, I hope, your enthusiasm to join them. Now it's time to take a more detailed personal inventory.

A personal inventory is a list of what you have learned to date in your life. This is the beginning of your harvest of self-knowledge. Completing a personal inventory will help you to acknowledge the new developments in your life and to recognize the constants that together make up the one and only you.

It is interesting how self-awareness works. It expands our point of view and opens our hearts and minds—because, I believe, it gives us a framework that supports us through the experiences to come. This framework provides a sense of safety and security, the same sureness you've heard the Women of the Harvest describe. As our sense of self grows we become, not more solid, static, and stuck in perspective as you might expect, but rather more light, flexible, and able to bend with what life brings. By moving your self-knowledge from tacit to explicit, you make it a more powerful ally for the rest of your journey.

As our sense of self grows we become, not more solid, static, and stuck in perspective as you might expect, but rather more light, flexible, and able to bend with what life brings.

These sorts of exercises can take courage. I believe the Women of the Harvest learned the most about themselves from reflecting on their toughest memories. But remember that the eyes with which you look at these events now have changed too, and the new perspective they offer will ease you through the rough spots.

The first inventory exercise is focused on what I call your *Been There Wisdom*. It's deceptively simple: you begin by thinking about what you have learned by living (fill in the blank) years. It can take any form—a narrative, a list of points, or just a series of words and ideas whose connections aren't clear to anyone but you.

My Been There Wisdom follows below. Write yours before or after you read mine. There is no right or wrong answer, just your ongoing discovery of your self.

Your Been There Wisdom
What do I know now that I did not know when I was younger?

Jaki's Been There Wisdom
I know that men are different from women, not better or worse, just different, and I only get in trouble when I forget this.

I was shocked the first time I realized that someone did not like me. But, if you live long enough, this will happen, and I know I never intended to hurt anyone.

I know that true friends do not judge you . . . they listen. Then, when you ask, they tell you honestly what they think and feel. They do not hold you accountable to live by their standards. They value you because you are different from them. Thank you to my true friends.

I know that values are not what your parents taught you.

They are not what you say you believe in or want to believe in.

They are what you do. Your actions show your values much clearer than your words.

I know that more often than not, when you ask a man what he is thinking and he responds, "Nothing," he is not lying. Though I don't know how they can sit there for hours and not have a single thought . . . about the relationship!

I know that good people do bad things and bad people do good things and you just can't make those labels stick on people.

I know that younger women are thinner than older women. However, it has nothing to do with hormones. It is because sooner or later you realize that there is just too much good food and wine in the world to make being thin worthwhile.

I know that no one loves you quite like your dog does . . . it is unconditional love and a truly rare human experience.

I know that no matter how much money you make or how much corporate power you have, you are never immune to the fears and insecurities that have haunted you since childhood.

I know that my fears are not real. They only exist in my head. I am still afraid of all those things because I am still using this head. But at least I know what is real and what is not.

I know that when you travel a lot, you give up most of the ideas you had about how people ought to live.

I know that when you lose your parents, the pain never goes away. It just becomes part of the flavor of you.

I know no one ever wrote music as beautiful as the morning birdsong.

I know that when you have children, you never stop loving them. No matter how many tattoos they get and no matter what political party they support.

I know that just because you rediscovered your physical self at 50, that does not mean your children want to hear about your sex life.

I know that sisters can be completely infuriating. However, you will still agree to meet them for coffee and you will still find something silly to share with laughter.

I know that happiness is the best cosmetic, and it is free. It may not always be in stock, but you can trust that another shipment is on its way.

I know that now, I do not want to live as they taught me in kindergarten but as they teach me in yoga class. With each breath, I approach life as if for the very first time.

This was written for BTW-LA, an organization for women 50+ based in Los Angeles, California, and the term

"Been There Wisdom" is used with their permission. Check it out at www.bigthinkingwomen.com.

Women of the Harvest Interview Questions

You can continue to reap your wisdom by answering the same questions I asked the Women of the Harvest in my interviews. The questions can be found in the Appendix at the back of this book.

I recommend you do this exercise by having a good friend ask you the questions. An objective interviewer can help you to reach a deeper level in your answers by probing for clarity and making you think harder than you would on your own.

> *There is not one life that does*
> *not have value when viewed with an open*
> *heart and uncritical eyes.*

If you are one of those women who have a formal-exercise phobia, then just sit down and think a while. You will need some quiet space and a pen and, most importantly, a pair of uncritical eyes and an open heart. Chances are you will discover both those things among the fruits of your harvest, so you will be able to give yourself a non-judgmental review. I promise you will be amazed and pleased with what you find. There is not one life that has come this far that does not have value when viewed with an open heart and uncritical eyes.

AFTER PAUSE, PRESS PLAY

So you have gathered the first fruits of your harvest. Now what? What can you do with this bounty?

To answer, let's go back to anthropology for a moment.

In a review of Sarah Blaffer Hrdy's *Mothers and Others: The Evolutionary Origins of Mutual Understanding*, Claudia Casper wrote in Toronto's *Globe and Mail*, "It has never been more important to understand human evolution. Without this understanding, we can never fully know our limitations or our strengths as a species, or hope to separate what is probable in our future from what is possible or impossible."

In understanding our evolution we substantially increase our ability to accept what and who we are and how we operate. Remember our parallel between the human female 50+ and the lioness and female baboon that outlive the birthing and rearing years? If we look back to the question we posed in chapter 1, we can begin to build an argument for the postmenopausal woman's role in society and the practical value of her wisdom.

Occasionally a lioness or a female baboon will also outlive the one- or two-year milestone. When this happens and the female is left with no offspring of her own who require her immediate attention, there is evidence that she takes on a new role in the pride or band as a community caregiver. These animal seniors become wise old aunties of sorts who pick up the chores that the more role-oriented youth don't have time for, caring for orphans, cleaning up the feeding grounds, and picking out the nits for the mateless. In a world that revolves around hunting and eating, surviving predators and disease, and breeding to keep the race viable, these "aunty" chores are quite important.

"So what of the female human?" we asked. "What is her role in these years past the span of her original design?" Well, for the lioness, protecting the pride is legacy creation, and that is exactly what we are to do with our wisdom harvest: build our legacy. The Women of the Harvest, each in their own way, are living and leaving a legacy that enriches their lives and the lives of those around them.

Your legacy can be the way you interact with your family in your own kitchen, the care you give to your most intimate relationships, or your work in your community . . . as big or as small as you are comfortable making it.

I'm not suggesting that you need to ramp up for the public podium or find your own private way to save the world in order to earn the right to call yourself a Woman of the Harvest. Some women I interviewed were doing exactly that, world-saving in its traditional form, while others were having just as important an impact in the much smaller circle of their families and friends. Your legacy will be a product of your self-knowledge and wisdom but also of your personality and the circumstances of your life. It can be the way you interact with your family in your own kitchen, the care you give to your most intimate relationships, or your work in your community . . . as big or as small as you are comfortable making it.

What matters is that the attitude with which you view life has been enriched by what you have come to appreciate about yourself. From that will flow the legacy that is uniquely yours.

In the legacy-creation business, sometimes the greatest challenge is being heard or accepted as a legacy maker. I think older women in particular face that challenge in our society. The Women of the Harvest often work alone in their fields and gardens. They spoke to me about feeling that they were now in places in which society in general had not previously been interested. But if we apply the demographics to the harvest metaphor, we must see that we have a bumper crop of wisdom on our hands. Can we really, on this planet, where each day a new resource is labeled endangered or unsustainable, afford to turn our backs on the bounty before us?

Now the numbers are in our favor. There's a double meaning there: the older you are the more wisdom you have, so your voice is emboldened with that wisdom, and we have mass on our side, so that voice is louder simply because there are more of us.

Maybe you don't see yourself as a legacy maker. I can assure you that many of the women I interviewed did not either. They were just living and legacy happened. Legacy makers don't require an extrovert personality or great riches or a large support staff to carve out their contribution to life. They come in all shapes and sizes, some quite surprising.

*Maybe you don't see yourself as a legacy maker.
I can assure you that many of the women I
interviewed did not either. They were just living
and legacy happened.*

Many years ago I had the pleasure of arranging for Bill O'Brien, the one-time CEO of Hanover Insurance, to speak at a conference that I was involved in organizing.

At the time I met Bill, he was a partner in a consulting firm. When he came to speak to our leadership conference, I sat nervously at the back of the room, having assumed a lot of responsibility for the success of this speaker.

Bill was an older gentleman with a soft voice. He did not use fancy audiovisual aids, just a flip chart that he often blocked from view with his body as he spoke. He turned away from the audience many times to scribble somewhat unintelligibly on this flip chart. He was breaking all the rules of perfect speaker form, and I was starting to panic. I began to envision the conversation in which my boss would ask me to explain exactly what I was thinking when I selected this man as our keynote speaker.

Then I noticed something. We were about five minutes into the presentation—yes, all that panic on my part happened within the longest five minutes of my working life—when it became apparent to me that Bill O'Brien held that room in the palm of his hand. You could have heard a pin drop. Two hundred and fifty people were under his spell. In my worry about his soft voice and old-fashioned flip chart, I had underestimated the power of wisdom to capture the heads and hearts of an audience. The delivery was not important because the content, the spirit, had captivated the room.

Please remember this story when you wonder if you can make a contribution.

Given what I saw that night, I was not surprised when I later ran across a paper Bill O'Brien had published in which he introduced a concept he called *Legacy Leadership*.

Bill described Legacy Leadership as the final stage of evolution in leaders' development—the time in their lives when they become more concerned with what they are giving back to their co-workers, customers, shareholders, and communities than with what they are getting from them. It is the time when leaders acknowledge how vast their impact can really be—when they accept the greater responsibility and the tougher challenge of impacting the entire lives, not just the livelihoods, of everyone who comes in contact with their organizations.

I think that what Bill described is indeed the natural evolution of all our human roles. The Women of the Harvest are nothing if not legacy leaders, and it is legacy leadership that will call us as we follow their path.

Each new Woman of the Harvest offers society a valuable example of the style and grace and contagious energy that can be awoken in a woman's life 50+. When I completed the interviews with these women, I knew that I needed to share what I had heard because it was something all women young and old needed to know. I had a strong urge to gather up the interviewees and hit the road to seats of government across the world shouting, "Listen up, folks!"

Think about the value that such wise women could be to themselves, their immediate circle, and collectively to society. Imagine a world enriched by actions that are shaped by this view of the world:

Enriching the world starts one person at a time, so as you read the following list, find yourself in each attribute of the Women of the Harvest.

How have you experienced each one?

How can the awareness of these experiences inform and nourish the rest of your life?

Femininity

Femininity starts at birth and continues till death; it is not defined by the tampon years. It is a glorious accident of birth and chromosome mix that cannot be lost because it is a woman's very nature—a nature with many outward faces culturally defined and shaped, but all just as they should be. In such expanded self-knowledge we can celebrate both the individual and all sisters sharing their birthright.

Desire

Time may run out for some things in life—success in business and a chance to raise a family, for example. But the end of a particular time can be a door, not a wall—a door that releases us from the theory of set patterns in life, releases us into the spontaneous flow of life.

At 40 you may be a CEO with responsibility for 26,000 people and then at 80 you may not have hierarchical authority over anyone or anything, but are you less valuable? Are you enjoying life less? It all depends if you have opened that next door or if you are standing there banging your head against the old wall. Wisdom tells us to do as seemingly powerless infants do: keep growing and see where it takes you.

The end of a particular
time in your life
can be a door, not a wall.

The "things" of life—roles, goods and property, reputation and awards—are time-bound and time-defined. To be able to let them slip into and out of your hands without grasping or regret is grace.

There is something perfect in our sense of timing when we can let go of the desires of a lifetime and experience not loss, but freedom . . . not an ending, but a new beginning.

Wisdom

We develop a reservoir of knowing over our lifetime and we can draw from it every day. In fact, as long as we draw breath we can draw wisdom. It comes from a well that is continuously filling up with life's experiences. No day and no event, good or bad, is ever left as waste, but becomes the recycled resource for our future. The Women of the Harvest know in their wisdom that as they age, time makes better use of them. If there is less time left, it is okay, because each moment is fuller of what matters.

*The Women of the Harvest
know in their wisdom that as they age,
time makes better use of them.*

Safety

The ultimate personal safety is the realization that you are comfortable in your own skin. You no longer need the approval of others or any other external validation to make you feel good about yourself. So many women wait expectantly for someone or something outside themselves to complete them and make them feel safe, when all along they had everything they needed to be whole. When you realize this, the power that others had to hurt you is gone. You are safe, safe to speak the undressed truth that before you might have swallowed in fear. Here's the irony: everyone else around you is made so much safer by that truth as well.

Trust

To let go of the promise that others will act just as you expect or as they have promised . . . to live comfortably knowing that neither you nor your closest partners can control this life . . . this is the trust of the harvest.

So often we define *trust* to mean that things will not change from how they are now or from how we imagine they should be. We put our "trust" in others to make sure that the world stays as it should be, we "trust" ourselves to act in ways appropriate to our beliefs, and we put our "trust" in God or the universe to maintain the order we believe in. Then when something happens outside our plan, usually something bad, we are not only injured and hurt; we are outraged, because this should not be, we "trusted" this would not happen.

The trust of the harvest comes from being released from the need to keep life unchanged. We replace that false sense of control with the understanding that peace and contentment does not come from a life free of pain, struggle, and challenge, but that the seeds of peace and contentment are sown by acceptance. When acceptance helps you redefine trust in your life, the ride will be a lot smoother, even over the bumpiest roads.

Selfishness

Selfishness is okay. It is better than okay, it is good. The word *selfishness* at its simplest really means "having self." Females are genetically programmed to put the needs of others, rather than of self, first. This characteristic was very likely programmed into the female genes for sound biological reasons. We are the breeders, and to perpetuate the species we must put the needs of the sperm donor and then the needs of the offspring first. It's simply required for the creation and survival of the next generation.

So wouldn't it then follow that after the fertile years, when the utility of this self-sacrifice is over, a woman should be able to get in touch with her selfish side?

The most interesting thing we discover about selfishness is its consequences. When you put your needs first, everyone benefits, not just you. Needs are honestly stated and actions uncomplicated by guilt filters.

Women do not run amok finding their inner bitches and making life miserable for everyone because, damn it, they have earned the right. Far from it. In selfishness, self-knowledge and wisdom speak clearly and from open hearts and the results are simple, direct, powerful, and kind.

Henry James wrote in *The Tragic Muse*, "One is one's self a fine consequence."

When we are "selfish"—when self-knowledge and wisdom speak clearly and from open hearts—the results are simple, direct, powerful, and kind.

Tolerance

Tolerance is found growing where previously judgment had choked it out. If you travel a lot and experience the habits and patterns of other cultures, you learn to give up your ideas about how others ought to live. We are all life travelers, even if we have never left our hometowns. As we live, we observe, and when we observe from the perspective of harvest abundance, we see that others are different people who deserve our respect and from whom we can learn.

We begin the journey to tolerance by seeing and rejoicing in our own uniqueness and our own unique contribution to this planet.

Then we see the uniqueness of others, their shapes and colors and their own inescapable and essential contribution. From this point of view we live and let live with dignity and integrity on all sides.

What impact might this vision have on power struggles, environmental issues, and human rights?

How could it change our world?

Belonging

Women of the Harvest walk with a strong step that says, "I have arrived and I have a right to be here. I belong here, wherever I am."

Their gait is erect and proud, but it can be difficult to appreciate. You will need to look past the bend in an older woman's back or the shuffle of a weakened foot as it scrapes the ground to see that each step resonates deep inside and leaves an imprint that rocks the earth around it. Diamonds on the soles of your shoes, baby!

We are all life travelers, even if we have never left our hometowns.

Gratitude

It gets no better than this. The perspective of gratitude is as close as we get in this life to being godlike, whoever or whatever our god may be.

A perspective of gratitude is the trifocal of aging eyes: expansive, ego-destroying, and peaceful.

Wonder

Life slows us down as we age, not to take the sprint from our last mile but to bring us back to wonder. It takes a two-year-old an hour to traverse a 30-foot strip of sidewalk. Children's senses explore every minute experience that arises in the moment. They do not have much past to drag around or many expectations to pull them away; they simply live now.

Wonder becomes available once again in aging. At both ends of life's continuum, time is focused naturally on the present. As the child has less past, the Women of the Harvest have less future, and as the child has few expectations for the future, the Women of the Harvest have given up their hopes for a better past.

So they share a preference to focus on the here and now—but unlike children, the light of wonder in the eyes of the Women of the Harvest is not naiveté. It is wisdom, and with that wisdom they live fully present and curious in the wonder of each moment. So fully present that there is little space available within which to cultivate regret and fear.

*Life slows us down as we age,
not to take the sprint from our last mile but to
bring us back to wonder.*

*Could we benefit from putting gratitude and
abundance ahead of greed? How about rethinking
the meaning of trust and counting only on change?
What would that do to our fear?*

What do you think—could any of this be useful today? We inhabit a planet where cultures are knocking up against each other more violently every day. Could we do with a little less judgment and a little more acceptance in our lives? Could we benefit from putting gratitude and abundance ahead of greed? How about rethinking the meaning of trust and counting only on change? What would that do to our fear? Could we love bigger and better if we did so in a spirit of peace and personal confidence?

I think we all know the answers to those questions (and I am sure you can hear John Lennon singing "Imagine" somewhere in the background as you read this). But there are people who live this way now. People who embrace life with open arms, whatever it may bring. You have met them in this book. You may now realize that you are one too. I can't wait to hear what your legacy will be.

For Your Reflection

If you haven't already done so, take some time to do the Been There Wisdom exercise. As you reflect on what you know now that you didn't know then, have you discovered anything that surprises you?

Answer the interview questions in the Appendix, working with a friend to "interview" you if possible. Did you turn up anything unexpected in that process?

What change do you think your knowledge harvest can bring about in your life? In the world?

CHAPTER 8:

The Coming of Age of Grace

Wwe all want to live longer. The most basic human desire, after all, is survival. So we pop the vitamins, work out at the gym, and pass on the cheesecake in the hope that life will not only continue, but continue with quality. We do continue, past 50 to 60, on to 70, then 80, and even 90 or more. The Women of the Harvest have popped the vitamins, worked the treadmill, and passed on the cheesecake like everyone else, and quite a few of the women I interviewed were well over 80. They have been fully engaged in all the years 50+ and now in their most senior years they are wide open and ready to enjoy what life has in store for them.

As we approach the eighth decade it becomes more difficult to maintain our faith in the perfect design of the female human machine. Our effort to forestall the body's decline will start to lose ground more quickly, as will our efforts to keep the world around us, the large or the small circle, just the way we like it. Inevitably, there will be losses. We needn't despair, though, because the Women of the Harvest have one final message for us.

Along with elegance, ladies, we have grace.

The grace to know that there are some things we cannot change is called *acceptance*, and, not coincidentally, this is the primary characteristic of the Women of the Harvest 80+. It is as if finding your way home begins with finally accepting first yourself and then the world around you. If you are ever going to add an attitude of acceptance to your life view, it will likely be in your eighth, ninth, or tenth decade.

> *Finding your way home*
> *begins with finally accepting first yourself*
> *and then the world around you.*

AN ACCEPTABLE TIME

Some people do not like the word acceptance; they think it means giving up or resigning oneself, usually to a horrid fate one has given up the fight to control. Poor word—it gets such a bad rap. Acceptance is not simply passive or active. In its most extreme form it is the ability to fight to the death for or against something and in that last breath to know the outcome could have been no other way. But acceptance can be considered passive, because you cannot make yourself accept but acceptance can come all the same.

Acceptance does not preclude trying to change things you don't like about yourself or the world. Rather it includes that effort as right action regardless of the results. And it doesn't preclude complaining about the things you don't like. Don't imagine I am describing a docile porch swing full of blissed-out 90-year-olds. These gals may well be the cantankerous, rowdy ones. That sparkle in their eyes is pure energy, and remember, they don't really care if you approve or not!

Acceptance is a natural extension of all the other characteristics of the Women of the Harvest and it encompasses all the other characteristics. The attitude of our heroines is rooted in their ability to receive into their lives as true whatever may come, respond as their nature dictates, and then receive that response as true, too.

Some may call this ability faith. The word you use to describe it will vary based on the framework you apply to understand it and the story you tell yourself about where it comes from. When acceptance is present, the words do not matter. Acceptance is a release from firmly held beliefs that we imagined defined us but actually confined us. These beliefs restricted the world we experienced like a narrow-angle lens. When acceptance happens, we get the freedom to see a wider-angle view of life. In that view, many of the rules of proper behavior disappear because they simply don't make sense anymore. We see that they hold us back from engaging in what we have really come to value in life.

Don't imagine that I am describing a docile porch swing full of blissed-out 90-year-olds. These gals may well be the cantankerous, rowdy ones.

Acceptance nurtures courage by revealing the connective tissue between us and others. We begin to accept others as they are, because the weight of judgment is lifted off our shoulders. No wonder the chest, home to the heart, sags: it is sheer relief to no longer hold the responsibility of keeping everyone in order. (This explains why grandparents seem just fine with some of the things their grandchildren do which, we know without a doubt, they would not have tolerated in their own children.)

Acceptance also changes our social landscape. We have more need for quiet time to reflect alone, and we have much less need to do what is required as opposed to what is truly desired.

And acceptance affects vision. As we age, we may see the surface of things less clearly (such as the small print in a newspaper), but we also begin to see below the surface with much more *in-sight*. Eventually we can hold two opposing things as true. We may find, for example, that we are able to see two sides of a disagreement between friends. I must warn you, this is not always popular. Often people want you to pick a side. But with the deeper insight of acceptance you may clearly see the point of view on both sides.

Perhaps we learn to do this because the longer we live and the more we experience, the less able we are to fit things into neat packages, so eventually we give up the effort and lose the urge and live more comfortably with ambiguity. We actually start to see the difference and the similarity of two distinct things at the same moment, as if accepting the differences reveals the common denominator of all things. This knowledge may have been available to us all the time, but we were too busy sorting, categorizing, and evaluating to see it. All things come in their own time.

The longer we live and the more we experience,
the less able we are to fit things into neat packages,
so eventually we live more comfortably
with ambiguity.

THE WALLS COME DOWN

Acceptance and self-awareness breed confidence and the ability to embrace yourself just as you are, with your likes, dislikes, quirks, and talents. You start to find yourself at home in your own skin.

Acceptance brings the peace to live life as it flows without the tension and effort of trying to make it what we believe it should be. Maybe we are helped into this stage by our failure to control the physical changes of aging. We can do a pretty good job up until our late 70s, but then it gets more difficult, and eventually we just have to yell out, "Okay, I give in!"

The Women of the Harvest know
that pain always changes the landscape,
and then there is something new to see.

Life contains a lot of things that hurt—things that are painful and difficult to see and experience. Such is the balance of living. Without this pain we would not recognize joy. The Women of the Harvest know that if you spend all your energy resisting what you don't like, laying blame and trying to reject the right of such things to exist, you will have little energy left to enjoy the things you do like. Instead they suggest that you hold one another up through the pain. They know that pain always changes the landscape, and then there is something new to see.

It is a fact of life that in this day and age an older woman will likely find herself alone later in life. That's just the way the statistics have worked out—divorce and life span and so on. But when acceptance has taken root, particularly in a woman over 80, she is able to stand alone, not immune to pain, but with comfort because she knows that there's really no such thing as alone.

When we are younger, we build walls around ourselves. These walls keep in the things we want and keep out the things we think we don't want and we have some pretty clear ideas about which is which.

These walls are the job descriptions of the roles we play, the rules of the society we belong to, the beliefs about life we have formed. Our sense of right and wrong is built into the walls; so are the people we approve of and the people we don't. We even shore them up with the tough, hard bodies that we sweat over at the gym. (Maybe it is called resistance training for a reason.)

And then we start to go soft.

You have read what the Women of the Harvest had to say. Did you hear the walls coming down in their words? The fortunate among us are not left vulnerable and alone when these walls crumble. Even if outward circumstances indicate otherwise, inside us acceptance provides a reassuring awareness like a companion that never leaves our side.

We have at this point befriended knowledge. As the walls start to come down, we become clearer not only about ourselves but also about where we fit in the world around us. As I mentioned earlier, we begin to sense the connective tissue that binds each of us one to the other.

THE OPEN FIELD

In the process of interviewing the remarkable Women of the Harvest, I saw a natural pattern begin to emerge. Each stage of a woman's life was perfect unto itself and the arc of life was one of transcendent transformation!

As the Women of the Harvest work, talking and writing, running and climbing, designing and innovating, nurturing and lobbying, and, most importantly, wondering, a transformation is happening naturally within them. The process that began at 50 continues, and as they approach their 80s they have become even lighter inside and out. It is as if they are dropping the weight of living quite naturally.

In the process of interviewing these remarkable women, I saw a natural pattern begin to emerge. Each stage of a woman's life was perfect unto itself and the arc of life was one of transcendent transformation!

They have gathered their wisdom harvest, shared it, and embraced it in their own lives. Now the field has been cleared, and the space that remains is far from barren. It is a space of pure potential, the most fertile ground a female ever knows.

I discovered this after all the interviews were completed, when I plotted out the answers by age and geographical location. I found no significant differences based on geography. But I was taken completely off guard when the age pattern began to reveal this area of light, this space I began to call the Open Field.

This Open Field began to reveal itself in comments like these from the Women of the Harvest:

"I feel this space starting to develop in my life. I find myself driven to arrange things so that there is more time between events, to give this space the room it may need to develop."

"I have found freedom in the failures of my life."

"Time makes better use of me."

"I don't have to be right all the time anymore . . . life is bigger now."

"One does not close down as one gets older; instead aging for me is about the discovery of life that is not the fertile woman."

"As you lose things, physical things and roles in life, the essential person becomes more apparent."

"In growing older you grow from limited vision to limitless vision . . . so many boundaries disappear."

"Life is a journey from and to freedom."

*The field has been cleared,
and the space that remains is the most fertile
ground a female ever knows.*

I had already been amazed at the power and strength I saw developing in women between 50 and 75, but when the trend turned deeper, turning toward peace, I was fascinated. I had not manipulated this discovery in any way with my interview questions, because I truly had no idea this was where we were going. But when we look at what the Women of the Harvest have shared with us, there is no denying the direction of their journey. When we track the changes over time from youth to the oldest age, we discover a progress from the outer world of stimulation, attraction, and drive to an inner world much more silent, peaceful, and accepting.

As I studied the Open Field, I wondered if it actually exists in all of us but most of us just don't discover it. I don't have an answer for that. I do know that not all people find their Open Field, and I know that for those who do, it has something to do with what I would call Presence. There are many definitions for this word, but in my lexicon *Presence* is the state of being completely one with all that exists. This is the state which exists when all the walls between you and everything else have come down and the Open Field is open to you.

I do not believe there is one universally correct definition or meaning for the experience of Presence. It is—perhaps ironically, since it describes a oneness—a completely personal and unique experience. When you have it you will make what you need to make of it.

Many years ago I was fortunate enough to attend a concert performed by Ofra Harnoy, the accomplished Canadian cellist. About two minutes into a piece, Harnoy closed her eyes and it seemed to me that she and the music had become one. This is Presence and the impact on performance is stunning. The artist is often unaware of what has happened in that space because she, the conscious part of herself, is absent.

It is as if the heavy matter of the artist, the chunky, bony, fleshy part, the needling, worrying, mental part and the fearful, arrogant, emotional part have merged into the music and the music flows through the shell, the body, which remains seated. I am not sure how it remains seated—imagine how light that body has become without all the weighty encumbrance of humanness!

You cannot create an experience of Presence, but if you have ever had one you may very well dedicate the rest of your life to trying to recreate it.

I believe this experience is not limited to performers in music; all sorts of people have such experiences. A teacher asking just the perfect question to draw out knowledge from within a student, but realizing afterward that he has no idea where that question came from; a surgeon knowing exactly how to move the scalpel, but being unable to connect that decision with any explicit knowledge that directs her hands.

You cannot create an experience of Presence, but if you have ever had one you may very well dedicate the rest of your life to trying to recreate it. It is a gift—one that, as luck would have it, seems to come more frequently with age. Why not? After all, the heavy matter is getting lighter and the space inside that holds the weightlessness has expanded . . . so bring on the music!

THEORY MEETS WONDER

Some time after I had completed my interviews with the Women of the Harvest and had the surprise of discovering what I called the Open Field, I came upon the work of Professor Lars Tornstam of Uppsala University in Sweden. Professor Tornstam's extensive research with men and women over 80 has identified a positive developmental

EXACTLY WHERE I AM SUPPOSED TO BE

There is an open field where I can go to play.

The ground is soft there and I can walk even on my stiff old legs.

There is no fence around this field to fence me in or to keep others out. So in this space I can be whatever and whoever I fancy in the moment.

There is no entrance gate or exit sign and I am not really sure how to get there or when to go.

There are no hours posted in this place. Time just does not seem to matter there.

I feel strong on the open field, sometimes bursting with grown-up wisdom and other times tickled by childish wonder.

I invite my very best friends to come there with me and we talk long into the night, words that reach so deep they touch our souls.

I feel at home on the open field, which is strange, as I don't think I have been there very many times before. But when I am there it is clear that it is exactly where I am supposed to be.

possibility he calls *gerotranscendence*. In *Gerotranscendence: A Developmental Theory of Positive Aging*, Professor Tornstam defines gerotranscendence as "a shift in metaperspective from a materialistic and pragmatic view of the world to a more cosmic and transcendent one." He has found evidence that "aging can entail a positive transformation leading to, among other things, increased inner security, wisdom and greater overall well-being." During this developmental process, our view of our own existence, of life in general, and even of ourselves gradually changes. His research has shown that "the gerotranscendent individual typically experiences a new understanding of fundamental existential questions—often a feeling of cosmic communion with the spirit of the universe, a redefinition of time and space, life and death, and a redefinition of the self and relationships to others." This is a time in which we develop the ability to cross borders of all kinds.

Not so long ago, theorists in the field of human development believed that we "peaked" at around 20 years of age. Later on, Carl Jung and Erik Erikson (husband of Joan) proposed that human development does continue in adulthood, but some still disagree. Indeed, that's why Professor Tornstam began his research into gerotranscendence—to bridge what he saw as the gap between the prevalent theories in social gerontology and what he observed in some of his subjects.

*It is bad enough to be struggling
with your body and its decline, but to believe that
your very development as a human being has
stopped—that is devastating.*

If the theory that we stop developing before we reach old age was once prevalent and is still supported by some, then I think we are getting to the root of why we reject aging and devalue the aged. The irony is that the smartest among us will be most fearful: they value learning and growth the most. If they believe that no more development will take place in their senior years, then how could they possibly look forward to those years or embrace them when they get there? No wonder many people over 80 suffer from depression and a sense of hopelessness. It is bad enough to be struggling with your body and its decline, but to believe that your very development as a human being has stopped—that must be devastating.

How do we form our expectations of our life in old age? We look over the fence at our older neighbors and see the outward signs of decline. We add the theories on human development that we picked up in college or somewhere else along the way. Then we stir in the media message that old is ugly, pretty is good, so old is bad, and voilà! It is easy to see why even Barbie won't admit her age.

When we look over that fence, though, we need to remember that things are not always as they seem. Take the gerotranscendent adult's need for increased time alone. What may look like dysfunctional withdrawal, Professor Tornstam has found, is sometimes positive solitude. We should be careful of jumping to conclusions about what we are seeing, and we should examine the quality of the knowledge that informs our perspective.

If we have maintained a good level of self-awareness through a practice like the wisdom harvest or just an active curiosity about life, then we will have at least the personal knowledge we need to counter the theory that our development has stopped. As we observe and learn, we know we grow because we experience ourselves growing, and that is all the proof we need, our own experience.

THE NEXT STAGE

I think that the reality of gerotranscendence is the best news to come to an aging population since high-fiber muffins at McDonald's. (Excuse me, please, Professor Tornstam, I don't mean to make light of your contribution!) His research adds credibility to the voices of the Women of the Harvest, because there are striking similarities between the signs of gerotranscendence and the Open Field that appears at the far end of the harvest years.

I propose to you that in the lives of these wise women, even as the body has weakened and worn, this space of openness has matured, perhaps unnoticed and unlooked-for, but with a power of its own.

Professor Tornstam suggests that gerotranscendence is not dependent on a formal religious practice or belief system, and the Women of the Harvest say the same. We should not assume that we need to be interested in matters of spirit for this finding to enrich our lives. The development of the Open Field in the Women of the Harvest is a natural process, just like the earlier stages of their development, and we must acknowledge that it will happen for some women but not all.

The Women of the Harvest describe an Open Field that is without matter, growing formlessly and weightlessly inside, consuming with its nothingness the previous effort and struggle. It replaces the solid mass of life—the body, worry, fear—with comfort and ease.

Even though it is light, it is strong, and its strength carries the pain of aging bones and the heartaches of loss and regret.

Many Women of the Harvest at 80+
are still passionately engaged in their work
and their communities. It is not readily
apparent to those around them that they
are changing inside.

Perhaps older women move among us invisibly for this very reason—because of this openness that consumes them even as they continue to go about the activities of their lives. This is a transformation of emphasis, not of activity. The meaning in life changes but the action may not. Many of the 80+ Women of the Harvest are still passionately engaged in their work and their communities. It is not readily apparent to those around them that they are changing inside. It may not even be apparent to the women themselves, because each day they become more occupied just being.

As long as we continue to breathe, we will get older. We have evidence now that the years before us are rich with opportunities to grow and contribute and learn about aspects of life we cannot even really get our heads around until we are fortunate enough to blow out 80 or 90 candles.

Far from being about drying up and withering away, the next stage of life is about filling up with the incredible lightness of being . . . until the step to the ultimate lightness is only a final breath away.

What a perfect plan!

We all know, in our clearest moments, that we have a sort of pilot light in us, burning subtly but continuously, with the occasional flare-up. I suggest that when a Woman of the Harvest reaches her oldest years, that tiny flame flares up brighter and brighter. It is the same light that has sparkled in her eyes all along, and the heat from it comforts and inspires us when we get close enough. As the years pass, this light does not fade. It keeps getting brighter year after year until it is all there is, shining from an Open Field within.

AND NOW...
JUST GET ON WITH LIVING

Have you ever looked up the word *age* in a dictionary? Here is how Merriam-Webster's Online Dictionary defines age as a verb:

1: to become old: show the effects or the characteristics of increasing age
2: to acquire a desirable quality (as mellowness or ripeness) by standing undisturbed for some time (letting cheese age)

And here's its definition as a transitive verb:

1: to cause to become old
2: to bring to a state fit for use or to maturity

Hands down, I vote for definition number two in both of these cases.

So, after all that I've written in the passionate hope that my sisters (and some of my brothers) will shift their perspective on their advancing years and on the concept of age, it seems all I needed to do was look in the dictionary!

I realize that I am abusing the clarity of Webster's a bit by suggesting that we would be better served by viewing human aging as we view the aging of cheese.

Adopt the number-two definitions and the quality of your life will improve—I guarantee it. If you believe that age is *a desirable quality* (as in *ripeness*), you are bound to have much happier "milestone" birthdays. If you understand that quality is achieved by *standing undisturbed for some time*, your years leading up to those birthdays will be much better. And when you can look in the mirror in your ninth or tenth decade and see someone who is *fit for use*, well, that will undoubtedly have a positive impact on your morning.

Have you ever noticed how a woman who would never have told you her age at 55 or 65 is quite proud to tell you that she is 92? It's because she knows something you don't.

The Women of the Harvest are very special women— not so much because of what they have done but because they are blessed by the attitude toward life that shapes their view of each day. We may not all become like them, but understanding that they exist and seeing their perspective as an option can start us all toward our own harvest.

My hope is that simply understanding the way these women live can shift us from shame and dread of aging

A LIVING REMBRANDT PORTRAIT

At the gate to the Church of Saints Peter and Paul in
Petrodvorets (Peterhof), Russia, a small peasant woman
positions herself as an informal greeter. If you give her some
change she will give you a used information pamphlet or a
crumbled postcard, so for her the interaction is a business
transaction, not charity. I do not believe she is aware of what
she really has to offer, and I do not believe that any tourist has
the money to pay her what it is truly worth.

This woman is obviously very poor and perhaps homeless,
though one cannot imagine how she could survive a Russian
winter without some form of shelter. Her clothes are torn and
even in summer she is wearing multiple layers that suggest
she may not have anywhere to leave her few spare items.
She is disheveled but not dirty—just some earth beneath her
fingernails from honest work, as your grandmother might have
after a day in the garden. She is round enough to seem as wide
as she is tall, but it does not appear to be from fat, just her solid
Russian stock.

Her eyes are the most memorable. They shine like an infant's,
but she is not new to this world. They are as deep as the eyes
of a mystic, but she seems to claim no knowledge. When you

come upon this face, you are shocked for a moment; you will realize later that as you looked, you felt love and safety. You felt something so deep that you stood on the edge of an abyss from which, if you fell in, you would never return—but you were not afraid. You realize all this later as you wander on, because the experience is too overwhelming for thinking in the moment.

This woman appears to live completely in the present at the gate to the church, present only in the moment with you. She does not live in some time of former glory in Russian history or in some dream of a better life like the one for which her children may have left her.

When you look at her, you sense that hidden behind her eyes is a limitless glimpse of the universe. To our logical minds it is remarkable that a focus on one dimension, the present, could reveal all dimensions simultaneously and offer to this tiny impoverished woman the power and peace that kings and clergy have sought throughout history.

It defies time and weight and any other measure we know.

toward a place where we can celebrate it. We can even start lying about our age in the other direction if we want! Have you ever noticed how a woman who would never have told you her age at 55 or 65 is quite proud to tell you that she is 92? I used to wonder why this was. Now I understand that it's because she knows something I don't.

If you are fortunate enough to shift your perspective, you should know that after a short while you will no longer be conscious of the change. I imagine that those around you *will* see the difference, and if you're lucky, they will remind you. Mostly, though, you will just get on with living.

I am sure that many of the women I interviewed will be surprised if they read this book. They will not necessarily see themselves in everything that is written here.

Your perspective becomes the eyes with which you see the world, and the eye cannot see itself.

Someone really wise told me many years ago, when I was just a kid of 35, that the secret to peace in life was indeed very simple. It was all about how you looked at it. Well it took a few years and a group of amazing women to make that sink in, but I get it now—and I guess when you look at it that way your eyes just can't help but reflect the sheer joy of it all.

For Your Reflection

If you could look at your life from the perspective of acceptance, what do you think might change?

What are the walls in your life made of? Have you started to notice any shifts or cracks in them?

Can you sense anything like the Open Field—any new space of lightness or expansion—opening within you?

APPENDIX:
Interview Questions

DEMOGRAPHICS

1. Age

2. Profession

3. Work status: *retired / employed / in transition*

4. Marital status

5. Children: *yes or no / ages / natural or adopted*

STAGE OF MENOPAUSE

6. Which stage are you at? Check one and answer the detail question(s).

□ A. Perimenopause
   Definition: *The time leading up to menopause when a woman stops menstruating because of a loss of functioning of her ovaries. Average age in U.S.: 47.5. Usually lasts two to seven years.*

How long have you been in perimenopause?

☐ B. The event of menopause
Definition: *A single point in time when you go one year without menstrual bleeding. Average age in U.S.: 51.*

How long has it been since your last period?

☐ C. Postmenopause
Definition: *The time after the last menstrual period that lasts the rest of your life.*

How long have you been in postmenopause?

☐ D. Medical or other premature menopause

How old were you when you entered medical or premature menopause?

What were the circumstances?

EXPERIENCE OF LIFE

7. How do the practical aspects of your life today—
work, living situation, relationships, hobbies, friendships,
geography—differ from before menopause or five years ago?

8. In the past few years, what changes have you noticed in yourself? How have you surprised yourself? What have you remarked upon to yourself, your friends, or your spouse?

Consider changes in these areas:

a. Physical

b. Intellectual

c. Emotional

d. Relationships

9. What new forces do you perceive pulling you or pushing you, even gently, at this time in your life? Which pre-existing forces are stronger and more common now?

10. What roles do you play in life now (mother, wife, daughter, lawyer, teacher)?

11. What roles did you play in life before menopause or five years ago?

12. How do the current roles differ from the former ones?

OUTLOOK

13. Tell me about the vision you have for the rest of your life.

14. How does it differ from the vision you had when you were 40?

15. How has your perspective on life changed in the past few years?

16. What are you excited about today? What do you and your friends talk about? Where is your attention drawn? What are you passionate about?

17. What were you excited about when you were younger—at 20, 30, 40, 50, 60, 70, 80, 90?

18. What do you fear today?

19. What did you fear when you were younger?

20. Why is it better to be [fill in your present age] than 25, 35, or 45?

OBSERVATION

21. What do you have or know now that you did not have or know when you were younger?

22. What have you learned from your past and how does it guide you now?

23. If I asked you to write about the gifts you have received from menopause or aging, what would you write?

ACTION

24. What do you feel the need to do now or wish you could do now?

MESSAGE

25. I am writing this book to encourage other women to shift their perspective on menopause and female aging. What do you want to say that you have not already said, so I can share it with others?

BIBLIOGRAPHY

Anderson, Joan. *A Walk on the Beach: Tales of Wisdom from an Unconventional Woman.* New York: Broadway Books, 2004.

Balsekar, Ramesh. *Peace and Harmony in Daily Living.* Mumbai: Yogi Impressions, 2003.

Brizendine, Louann, M.D. *The Female Brain.* New York: Broadway Books, 2007.

Erikson, Joan M. *The Life Cycle Completed*, Extended Version. New York: Norton, 1997.

Lindbergh, Anne Morrow. *Gift from the Sea.* New York: Pantheon Books, 1991.

Liquorman, Wayne. *Enlightenment Is Not What You Think.* Redondo Beach, CA: Advaita Press, 2009.

Love, Susan M., M.D. Dr. *Susan Love's Menopause & Hormone Book.* New York: Three Rivers Press, 1997.

Pink, Daniel H. *Whole New Mind: Moving from the Information Age to the Conceptual Age.* New York: Riverhead Books, 2005.

Sheehy, Gail. *New Passages.* New York: Ballantine Books, 1996.

Sheehy, Gail. *The Silent Passage*, Revised and Updated Edition. New York: Pocket Books, 1998.

Shulman, Neil B., M.D., and Edmund S. Kim, M.D. *Healthy Transitions A Woman's Guide to Perimenopause, Menopause & Beyond.* New York: Prometheus Books, 2004.

Tornstam, Lars, Ph.D. *Gerotranscendence: A Developmental Theory of Positive Aging.* Boston: Springer Company, 2005.

Wadensten, Barbro, Ph.D., R.N. "Issue and Innovations in Nursing
    Practice, Introducing Older People to the Theory of
    Gerotranscendence." *Journal of Advanced Nursing* 52,
    no. 4 (2005): 381-88.

RESOURCES: MAGAZINES

More (U.S.)
www.more.com

Women & Home
www.womenandhome.com

Zoomer (Canada)
www.everythingzoomer.com

ONLINE COMMUNITIES

Big Thinking Women
www.bigthinkingwomen.com

Eons.com
The Online Community for BOOMers
www.facebook.com/EonsInc

wowowow.com
A New Way for Women to Talk Culture, Politics & Gossip
www.wowowow.com

fiftyfab.com
Explore Your Wisdom Harvest Further at
www.fiftyfab.com